Kaleidoscope of Knowledge: Unifying Perspectives

Editor

RAVI KUMAR BOMMISETTI

SPI PUBLICATIONS

Published by **SPI Publications**, www.spipublications.in

SPI, the **SPI logo**, and **Split Poetry India** are trademarks of **SPI Publications**, or its affiliates.

ISBN-13: 978-81-992622-5-6

First Edition 2025

SPI Publications

Corporate & Editorial Office
117/2, Sector 37, Khandsa Road,
Gurgaon, Haryana 122 001
Phone: +91 98355 52940
Email: contact@spipublications.in
Website: www.spipublications.in

Processed and Printed in India

Preface

We respect and value educators more than we do any other group of professionals. Few professionals, aside from a select few other civil servants like law enforcement and the military, put in as much effort as educators, offer such a vital service to society and get as little appreciation and pay as they do. To become and stay an exceptional educator, one must be a remarkable person. Becoming and staying an instructional and educational leader requires even greater dedication and sacrifice. I appreciate everything you do and hope that the knowledge I offer in this book will support your work and help you become more effective in many ways.

This book, "Kaleidoscope of Knowledge: Unifying Perspectives," emerges from the urgent need to address the complex challenges of research across various domains in the present era. Recognizing that no single discipline holds all the answers, this work brings together perspectives from diverse fields – including Social Sciences, Engineering, Sciences, and ethics etc… – to offer a comprehensive understanding of the issues at hand and potential solutions. The book's primary aim is to explore the connection of various disciplines under one roof. The journey of researching and writing this book has been a collaborative effort, involving contributions from experts across a variety of disciplines. I believe that by embracing a multidisciplinary connection, we can move beyond multidisciplinary silos and foster a more robust and effective response to the challenges of the research in all domains. We hope this book inspires readers to think critically, collaborate across disciplines, and contribute to a more sustainable and equitable future.

ACKNOWLEDGEMENTS

I would like to convey my heartfelt gratitude to the management of Akal University for their tremendous support and assistance in the completion of my Book. I would also like to thank our beloved Vice Chancellor, Prof. Dr. Gurmail Singh, Registrar, Prof. Sawarn Singh and Dean Academic Affairs, Maj. Gen. (Dr.) G. S. Lamba for providing me with this wonderful opportunity to work on a Book entitled "Kaleidoscope of Knowledge: Unifying Perspectives." The completion of the Book would not have been possible without their help and insights.

Special thanks to my family for their patience and understanding during the long hours spent immersed in academic pursuit. To my colleagues in the department, your intellectual camaraderie has been a constant source of inspiration.

From the bottom of my heart, I would like to extend my deep sense of gratitude to all the reviewers of various disciplines. I appreciate the time and effort of the reviewers' for providing the feedback on the manuscripts. I am also grateful for their insightful comments and valuable improvements to the book.

Table of Contents

About the Editor

Dr. Bommisetti Ravi Kumar, who authored various books in the stream of Commerce & Management, is a distinguished faculty member in the department of Commerce at Akal University, Punjab. He is versatile in multidisciplinary specializations in Management. He has rich experience in teaching & research and proved himself as an effective teacher. He did his Masters in M.Com-Finance, MBA-HRM. He is awarded with M.Phil degree from Periyar University and Ph.D. degree from Acharya Nagarjuna University, India for his work in the field of Human Resource Management in 2011. He is the recipient of "Excellence in Teaching and Research Award," "Best Faculty in Rural Institution Award," and "Outstanding Faculty Award," etc., from various reputed organizations.

He is one of the members of the editorial board to various reputed international and national SCIE/Scopus and refereed journals. His laurels include numerous peer reviewed publications in National and International SCIE/Scopus/UGC-CARE and ABDC Indexed Journals of repute. He has presented several papers in International Level Colloquiums and National Level Seminars. He delivered lectures and also acted as a chair person in various National and International Level conferences.

Dr. B. Ravi Kumar is recognized as a research supervisor for ICFAI University - Jharkhand, Shri Jagdishprasad Jhabarmal Tibrewala University – Rajasthan, Bharathiar University – Coimbatore, Pacific University – Rajasthan, and Visiting Faculty – cum -Research Supervisor for Apex Professional University – Arunachal Pradesh in the stream of Management. He is one of the members of various professional bodies like Indian Academicians and Researchers Association, Associated Asia Research Foundation, American Association of International Researchers - USA, International Society for Development and Sustainability – Japan, International Society for Research & Development – UK, etc.

The Attitude of Post-Graduate Students about the Execution of Research Activities at University Level

Mudasir Amin
Assistant Professor Akal University Talwandi Sabo Bathinda-Punjab India
E-mail: mudasiramin861@gmail.com

Abstract

Research is the scientific investigation of a problem in which the reliable and valid results are brought in front of the people. The main purpose of the research is the acquiring of knowledge, development of theories, and diffusion of knowledge. This study examined the attitude of Post-Graduate students towards research in central universities. The objectives of this research study is to measure the attitude of Post-Graduate students towards research and to compare the attitude of Post-Graduate students' towards research with respective to their gender, locality, and discipline.The study adopted the descriptive survey method. The sampling of the study was selected throughstratified sampling technique in which 196Post-Graduate students of social sciences and humanities have been selected. The data has been collected by using the standardised research tool i.e. Attitude Scale of Dr. Vishal Sood and Prof. Y.K. Sharma and the data was analyzed by the statistical technique mean, standard deviation, t-test, frequency and percentage count. The results of the study revealed that most of the Post-Graduate students have Unfavourable attitude towards research whereas very less percentage of students are having a favourable attitude towards research. No differences were found in the Post-Graduate students towards research in relation to gender, locality, and discipline. Therefore it is concluded that there is a same negative attitude of Post-Graduate students towards research either in gender wise, locality wise or discipline wise.

Keywords: Attitude, Research, Post-Graduate Students, Favourable, Unfavourable.

1. INTRODUCTION

"Education is the most powerful weapon you can use to change the World" (Nelson Mandela).According to Aristotle- "Education is the creation of sound mind in a sound body." Education is the only treasure which can be mugged. It helps to build internal as well as outer behavior, strengthens our mind and expands our pool of understanding.The word "educate" stand for a number of meanings that are synonymous and also covers a wide range, such as- to educate means to teach, to train, to instruct, to inform etc. One can say that learning is a part of education. So learning is the end product of the process called education. In other words education is the process by which an individual is encouraged to develop his talent. The process of education aims at the all-round development of individuals. It helps in enhancing the moral values in the society. It forms the bases for lifelong learning. Through education a person can acquire skills to become more self-reliant and to prepare a person to faces the day today challenges of the life. Education helps to make one's life easier and comfortable. To make people more responsible and well informed, education plays a major role in this context. The education is the key which allows people to open up the world of opportunities and get success in their life. Higher education plays an important role in the development of nation. It helps the members of the society to get lives, to develop well and to improve the strength of the nation. There is pursuit of truth and excellence in man and only the higher education can direct the right path of it.

1.1 Meaning of Research

The word "research" has its etymological roots in the French word "recherché," which means "to seek again." Finding new knowledge, the truth, and so forth using evidence-based methods is the essence of what investigations are truly about. Disseminating information and formulating hypotheses using credible data is its key objective. There's an overall shift coming from learning through sources such as customs, tradition, culture, authority, and experience to using investigations that follow the principles of science, although humans haven't yet developed a flawless method for solving problems that are deemed appropriate of discovery.Stated differently, research is an organized, rational, systematic, and exacting process that seeks to solve issues and find new information. One definition of research is the application of science to the study of problems. Some people use the phrases "research" and "scientific method" interchangeably. In order to continue a scientific approach of analysis to discover and develop an organized corpus of information, research is thought to be a more structured and systematic process. A controlled observation process combined with objective, unbiased, empirical, and logical analysis and recording can result in the development of theories, generalizations, and, to some extent, the prediction and control of events that may be causes or consequences of particular phenomena.

1.1.I Approaches of Research

i. Qualitative Research: The technique of inquiring that aids in a thorough knowledge of the topics or issues inherent in their natural environments is known as qualitative research. This research approach does not use statistics. The expertise of the investigators and the inquiries they employ to delve further into the participants are crucial components of qualitative studies. Open-ended questions are posed in this kind of study so that one inquiry leads to another. The goal of naturalistic investigation in qualitative research is to gain an in-depth knowledge of social occurrences in their natural environments. It depends on people's own observations as meaning-makers in their daily lives and concentrates on the "underlying" causes of social occurrences instead of the "what" that comes out of them. Numerous qualitative research methodologies are employed, including content evaluation, group discussions, ethnographic research, in-depth interviews, and case studies. Qualitative approaches yield more descriptive results, and the data readily allows for the drawing of conclusions.

ii. Quantitative Research:A systematic approach to gathering data and interpreting it to make inferences is known as quantitative research. This research method collects and analyzes data using a computational, statistical, and comparable approach, in contrast to qualitative research. The main focus of quantitative data is numbers. A big population is needed for quantitative research since more participants equals more data. In this way, more data may be examined in order to produce precise findings. Closed-ended questions are used in this kind of research methodology since the main goal of quantitative research is to measure the quantity and acquire evidence of statistical data. Gathering measurable data and applying statistical, mathematical, or computational approaches to systematically investigate phenomena is known as quantitative research. Through the use of sampling techniques and online surveys, polls, and questionnaires, quantitative research collects data from both current and future clients; the findings can be presented as numerical data. Having carefully considered these figures, one can forecast a product's or service's future and make adjustments in accordance with that forecast.

1.1.II Types of Research: In practice, three primary categories of research are encountered. They're (i) Fundamental or Basic Research; (ii) Applied Research; and (iii) Action Research

i. Basic Research: The primary goal of basic research is to advance knowledge. It addresses the foundational facets of research. The development of knowledge is the primary driving force behind this study. This research is non-commercial in nature and does not aid in the creation or invention of anything. For example, an experiment is a good example of basic research. **Fundamental research,** also knownas **basic research or pure research** does not usually generate findings that have immediate applications in a practical level. Fundamental research is driven by curiosity and the desire to expand knowledge in specific research area. This type of research makes a specific contribution to the academic body of knowledge in the research area.Fundamental studies tend to make generalizations about the phenomenon, and the philosophy of this type of studies can be explained as "learning things for the sake of learning them." Fundamental researches mainly aim to answer the questions of why, what or how and they tend to contribute the pool of fundamental knowledge in the research area.

ii. Applied Research: Applied research focuses on analyzing and solving real-life problems. This type of research refers to the study that helps solve practical problems using scientific methods. This research plays an important role in solving issues that impact the overall well-being of humans. For example, finding a specific cure for a disease. Applied research "aims at finding a solution for an immediate problem facing a society, or an industrial/business organization, whereas fundamental research is mainly concerned with generalizations and with the formulation of a theory" Applied research is considered to be non-systematic inquiry and it is usually launched by a company, agency or an individual in order to address a specific problem.

iii. Action Research: The idea of action research was put forward for the first time by Kurt Levin in 1946. The use of the word 'action research' was made by Stephen core in 1957 and the detailed description of action research was made by Lawrence Enhans in 1975 in his book entitled, "Teacher as a Researcher".Applied research includes action research as a subset. Action research and applied research are sometimes distinguished from one another by arguing that the former is only relevant in educational settings while the latter can go further into more complex and widely applicable practical issues. In India, a practitioner might be a classroom teacher, a school's principal or headmaster, a block education official, the inspector of schools, or a teacher-educator at the DIET (Teacher Training Institution) level.

1.2 Concept of the Attitude: The agreeable or disagreeable responses towards any class of stimulus like a nation, a human group, customs, thoughts or institution are called attitudes.In Allport's words from 1967, "an attitude is a mental and neural state of readiness, organized through experience, exerting a directive or dynamic influence up on the individual's response to all objects and situations with which it is related." "An attitude characteristically provokes behavior that is acquisitive, favorable or unfavorable, affirmative or negative towards the object or class of objects with which is related. This double polarity in the direction of attitudes is often regarded as their most distinguish.""Degree of positive or negative affect (i.e. feelings) associated with some object (symbol, slogan, individual, institution, etc.)" Thurston (1959).

2. LITERATURE REVIEW

The researcher for this purpose came across the following studies done in India and abroad on the various aspects of attitude of students towards research. The researcher has reviewed various studies conducted in the area of present study which enabled to think in the line of the study.

Elena C. Papanasatasiou (2005) conducted the research on “Factor Structure on the Attitude towards Research”. In this study Research Methodology courses are typically viewed unfavorably by undergraduate students. But in order to help teachers foster more favorable attitudes about these kinds of courses and help students learn about research, they must have a better grasp of these views. **Ahmad M. M. Abdel Hafez (2007)** Conducted in research on “Postgraduate Research Students’ Knowledge and Attitudes towards Good Supervisory Practice at the University of Exeter”. The results of this study showed a strong positive association between the attitudes Exeter University students have toward their supervisor and their understanding of the code of supervisory practice. Regarding gender and academic year, there were no disparities observed in the knowledge or attitudes of the students. The results also revealed,Positive relationships between students and supervisors will arise for mutual advantage if students are better informed about the code of supervisory practice. **Zarifian and Mohammadi (2009)** in their research titled: “Measurement of attitudes of students toward research and influencing factors: (Case study of students of Faculty of Agriculture throughout 2008-2009)” discovered that the tendency of students to study is significantly correlated with the usage of information resources, faculty members' attitudes toward research, availability to suitable research facilities, academic performance, attitude, discipline, curiosity, and family. **Shirbagi (2011)** came to the conclusion that female students are less concerned about the challenges of research than their male counterparts in his study titled "A Survey of Kurdistan University Postgraduate Students’ Attitudes to Research and Its Relationship with their Research Self-Efficacy." Furthermore, students from the faculty of technical and engineering had the highest positive attitudes about research. On the other hand, students in the Humanities faculty expressed greater fear when it came to conducting research. Students generally expressed low levels of fear about undertaking research and high levels of belief in the use and benefits of research activities in their future careers.**Dhrubajyoti Deka (2012)** conducted a study on “Attitudes of Post Graduate Students towards Research”. The study's findings indicated that postgraduate students tended to have a negative attitude towards research. **Jagminder Kaur (2015)** carried out research on “Attitude of PostGraduate Students towards Research”**.** The findings are i) Research is not seen favorably by the majority of post-graduate students. ii) The attitude towards research differs significantly between male and female post-graduate students based on their mean scores. Gender significantly influences post-graduate students' attitudes on research.iii) The mean scores of post-graduate students enrolled in government-aided and privately funded colleges on the attitude toward research variable do not differ significantly. The kind of school has no appreciable bearing on postgraduate students' attitudes on research. **Prema muthuswamy and R. Vanitha (2017)** conducted on research “A Study of Attitude Towards research among the Doctoral Students”.Six components related to attitude toward research were identified via factor analysis. The elements include a passion for research, a fear of research, the value and utility of research, its challenges, its significance, and its advantages. The availability of an intriguing project, desire to work in a top-tier research group, and interest in the topic area rank as the top three factors influencing their decision to enroll in a PhD program. **Samuel Adaboh, et.al. (2017)** conducted a research on “A Study of Student Anxiety towards Research in two Undergraduate Programmes in a Ghanaian University”.Despite smaller mean disparities in terms of research techniques complexity and research relevance to participants' lives, the results showed no statistically significant differences between students in the two program groups on the ATR.**Raj Kishore Koul (2018)**carried out research on “Attitude of Post-Graduate students towards Research”. The study's main conclusions were that attitudes toward research among PG students are not significantly different for males and females. However, postgraduate students from the

Science and Arts streams have very different attitudes. Once more, PG students enrolled in general courses and those in professional courses do not significantly differ in their attitudes toward research.

3. NEED AND SIGNIFICANCE OF THE STUDY

Research is the process of looking for answers to issues and locating relevant, high-quality information. Research identifies, clarifies, and assesses novel concepts, ideas, and technological advancements that will shape humankind's future. In order to provide exceptional student education and training, faculty members must be encouraged to pursue professional greatness through research. A curriculum that is current and relevant cannot exist without research. Research benefits future generations as well as you by improving services and treatments. It aids in the development of novel diagnostic tools, therapies, and procedures that may one day benefit your grandchildren or maybe your own children. However, it has recently been noted that the caliber of researchers across all degree levels is extremely low. As a result, the researcher hopes to foster a favorable attitude toward student research. Therefore, in order to help students learn about research and research-related activities, barriers to research could be removed. Few of them actually sign up for activities linked to research. The absence of research-related activity could be the cause. As a result, the researcher is curious about the postgraduate students' mentality and their level of research aptitude. The study's conclusions will be beneficial to the field of educational research. Therefore, there is a great need for and value of this study.

4. OBJECTIVES OF THE RESEARCH STUDY

I. To find out postgraduate students' attitudes regarding research at central universities.

II. To contrast postgraduate students' attitudes regarding research according to gender.

III. To contrast postgraduate students' attitudes about research with those of their locality of residence.

IV. To contrast postgraduate students' perspectives on research in relation to their discipline of study.

5. HYPOTHESES OF THE RESEARCH STUDY

I. Not every post-graduate student approaches research with the same mindset.

II. Male and female postgraduate students' opinions regarding research do not significantly differ from one another.

III. The views of postgraduate students living in rural and urban areas toward research do not significantly differ from one another.

IV. Regarding their discipline, post-graduate students' attitudes about research do not significantly differ from one another.

6. RESEARCH METHODOLOGY AND PROCEDURE

Descriptive survey methodology has been used for this investigation.The population of the current study consisted of all Post Graduate students at the Central University of Jammu and Kashmir, India, who are enrolled in different departments related to the social sciences and humanities. Under the umbrella of social sciences and humanities, seven departments have been operational. Using the stratified selection technique, a sample of post-graduate students at Central University of Jammu and Kashmir was selected for this investigation.Initially, the units were chosen through a stratified process involving all social science and humanities departments. A random selection of 50% of the post-graduate students in each department of social science and humanities was made using a study sample. 196 post-graduate students from the Central University of Jammu and Kashmir's social science and humanities departments made up the study's total sample. The researcher has given the research participants the adopted scale, which was created by Dr. Vishal Sood and Prof. Y.K. Sharma, after choosing the sample using stratified random sampling.

7. DATA ANALYSIS AND INTERPRETATION

While a variety of statistical methods might be applied to analyze the data, the focus of the current study was on post-graduate students' attitudes toward research in connection to their gender, discipline, and location. The data were analyzed and interpreted using statistical techniques such as mean, standard deviation, t-test, frequency, and percentage count.

Hypothesis 1: Not every post-graduate student approaches research with the same mindset.

Table 1 Postgraduate students level of Attitude towards Research (N=196)

S. No	Level of attitude	Number of students	Percentage
1.	Extremely favorable (196 above)	0	0%
2.	High favorable (184-183)	04	2%
3.	Above average favorable (172-183)	09	5%
4.	Moderately favorable (156-171)	49	25%
5.	Unfavorable (144-155)	77	39%
6.	High Unfavorable (132-143)	37	19%
7.	Extremely Unfavorable (131and above)	20	10%
	Total	**196**	**100%**

After employing the statistical techniques for analyzing the data, the level of attitude was observed categories into three level; 1.Extremely favorable level (i.e. 196 above), 2.Moderately favorable level (156-183), and 3.Extremely Unfavorable level (131 above). It can be seen from the Table 1 that out of 196 participants 77 (39%) participants were found unfavorable attitude towards research. The above table vividly shows the 25% of Postgraduate students of attitude was moderately favorable. When it observed the Postgraduate students attitude 19% of the participants were observed as highly unfavorable attitude towards research. It is observed that 10% of them were having unfavorable attitude towards research. 5% of them had found to have above average favorable attitude towards research and 2% of the participants were high attitude towards research. The findings one contradictory in the study done by Tariq Hussain, Mumtaz Akhter, Nisar Abid, and Sidra Sabir December (2016).The findings demonstrated that students see research with positivity. The findings indicated that there is little variation in the attitudes of male and female students toward research. Thus, it can be seen from the Table that majority of participants were found to have an unfavorable attitude towards research.

Hypothesis 2: Male and female postgraduate students' opinions regarding research do not significantly differ from one another.

Table 2 the gender-sensitive attitude score of post-graduate students toward research includes the mean, standard deviation, and t-value.

Variables		Frequency	%	Mean	SD	t-value	Level of significance
Gender	Male	45	22.96%	151.1	18.31	1.51	0.05
	Female	151	77.04%	147.1	14.41		

After the completion of scoring of the data, the raw data were analyzed through mean and using SPSS version. From the above Table2, it can be seen that the majority of the participants involved in this study were female 151 whereas male were 45. It can be interpreted, that the obtained t-value of 1.51 which is less than the Table value of 1.96 which is not statistically significant at 0.05 levels. Therefore, it can be concluded that The attitudes of postgraduate students are not significantly different based on their gender. Hence, it may be pointed out that hypothesis 1 stating, "There is no significance difference between the attitudes of male and female students of Post-Graduate towards research", is accepted at 0.05 level of significance. The contradictory findings were also observed study done by Sadia Shaukat (2014) conducted on research on "Post graduate students' Attitude towards Research". The findings showed that compared to females, males had considerably more positive attitudes regarding research. Faustino E. Oguan Jr. (2014)the study's conclusions showed that male students had higher levels of positivity than female students. An investigation into post-graduate students' attitudes toward research was carried out by Mr. Raj Kishore Koul (2018). The study's main conclusions were that views toward research among PG students, male and female, do not significantly differ from one another.

Hypothesis 3: The views of post-graduate students living in rural and urban areas regarding research do not significantly differ from one another.

Table 3 Post-graduate students' attitude towards research with respect to locality was measured using the mean, standard deviation, and t-value.

Variables	Locality	Frequency (N)	%	Mean	SD	t-value	Level of significance
Locality	Rural	124	63.27%	148.16	14.22	.080	0.05
	Urban	72	36.73%	147.98	17.42		

Table 3 reveals that the 63.27% of the participants were belonging to rural areas whereas 36.73% were as urban areas. The raw data was calculated as through SPSS version. Upon computation, the t-value came out to be.080, which is less than the 1.96 number in the table and not significant for significance levels of 0.05. Therefore, the hypothesis No. 2 the views of post-graduate students living in rural and urban areas regarding research do not significantly differ from one another has been accepted. Thus, it can be concluded that the urban and rural students were found to have no significant difference in the attitude towards research.

Hypothesis 4: Regarding their discipline, post-graduate students' attitudes about research do not significantly differ from one another.

Table 4 the mean, standard deviation, and t-value of postgraduate students' attitude score toward social science and humanities research

Variables		Frequency	%	Mean	SD	t-value	Level of significance
Discipline	Social science	123	62.76%	149.27	15.69	.853	0.05
	Humanities	73	37.24%	146.12	14.88		

From the Table 4 observed that the 62.76% of the students were belonging to social science discipline whereas 37.24% of them belonged to humanities. The Table indicates that majority of the participated students in the study were belonging to social science discipline. The raw data was calculated as through SPSS version. The obtained t-value was found to be .853 is less than the Table value of 1.96 and is not statistically significant at 0.05 level of significance. Therefore, there is no significant difference in the attitude of Social Science and Humanities discipline of

Postgraduate students towards research. Hence the Null Hypothesis is accepted. The dissimilar results found on the study conducted by Syed Noor-ul-Amin (2017). The findings of the study was Social Science and Arts stream found with a favorable Attitude towards Research as against to their comparable group.

8. MAJOR FINDINGS OF THE STUDY

The study's main conclusions, which came from the data's analysis and interpretation, are listed below.

- The study revealed that 39% of postgraduate students were found to have unfavorable attitude towards research whereas only 2% of them were having a highly favorable attitude towards research.
- It was found from the study that 25% of the Postgraduate students have a moderate attitude whereas 5% of them were having an average favorable attitude towards research.
- It was estimated from the study that 37% were found to have highly unfavorable attitude towards research whereas 5% of them were having a favorable attitude towards research.
- 25% of participants had a moderately positive attitude about research, according to the survey, whereas 19% of participants had a very negative attitude toward it.
- 10% of postgraduate students had a very negative attitude about research, according to the study.
- According to the study, the majority of postgraduate students had a negative attitude toward research.
- The survey concluded that there is no discernible gender difference in the attitudes of postgraduate students regarding research.
- According to the study, postgraduate students' attitude toward research was found to be similar whether they lived in an urban or rural region.
- The study demonstrated that postgraduate student's attitude regarding research in relation to their discipline did not significantly differ from one another.

9. DISCUSSION OF THE FINDINGS

The majority of postgraduate students in the current survey were found to have a negative attitude toward research. However, this result was in line with a study on "Attitude of students towards research" done in 2014 by Aminder Kaur. According to the study, the majority of students did not view research activities favorably. This study shown that most students' aptitude for and understanding of research activities fall short of expectations. It is evident that nearly all of the graduating students had a bad attitude about research, which is unfortunate since a country's advancement in research and technology is something that should be celebrated.The results of this study were also integrated into a study on postgraduate students' attitudes toward research that Jagminder Kaur (2015) did. According to the study, the majority of post-graduate students have a negative attitude about research.

The current study found a statistically significant difference in the mean scores of male and female post-graduate students on the attitude toward research variable. Postgraduate students' attitude regarding research is significantly influenced by their gender. Thus, the researcher recommends holding a variety of workshops, conferences, seminars, and lectures to help post-graduate students develop a positive outlook. Some pedagogical implications to instill the attitude in the pupils have been proposed based on the discussion of the primary findings.

10. SUGGESTIONS FOR THE FURTHER RESEARCH

Research is never ending process the more one plunges into the ocean of knowledge open for him/her. Researches, which are usually few in the field of education, cannot fall its entire problem.

Hence more and more research is required to be undertaken. Due to various obstacles/limitations with regard to key factors. Present investigation could not cover-up all dimensions of the topic. The following suggestions may be considered to undertake researches for this exploration.

1. The current study is confined to the postgraduate students of Central University of Jammu only. So, it can be replicated on the other universities of Jammu province.
2. In the current study, the sample size of the study is 196 Postgraduate students only. It seems to be a very small sample. Therefore, it can be undertaken in the large sample so that they may obtain more reliable and represents the actual status of attitude of postgraduate students.
3. In the present study, the investigator concentrated only on comparison of attitudes with regard to gender, locality and discipline. It can also be explored further by considering the other variables such as academic achievement and educational qualification etc.
4. The Study may be conducted to examine the correlation between the attitude (dependent variable) possessed and gender, locality, stream (independent variables).

11. EDUCATIONAL IMPLICATIONS OF THE STUDY

1. According to the study, 68% of postgraduate students had a negative attitude toward research. It is advised that in order to instill in students a good attitude toward research, all higher education institutions should host various workshops, seminars, conferences, exhibitions, etc.
2. The finding of the present study may be helpful for teachers, educational institutions, curriculum developers, policy makers, and researchers.
3. According to the current study, the majority of students do not have a good attitude toward research. As a result, it is important to foster a positive attitude in new researchers by providing them with workshops, orientation courses, and extended talks by renowned researchers, among other things.
4. The current study makes it clear that male students see research more favorably than do female students. It is also important to work on helping female researchers adopt a positive outlook on their work. To help them build a good attitude, postgraduate students may be introduced to short-term orientation courses.
5. Instructors ought to motivate their pupils to become aware of and comfortable with the significance of investigation.
6. Instructors should concentrate on putting higher authority's norms and regulations into practice in order to pique students' enthusiasm in conducting research.

12. CONCLUSION

The investigator looked into 23 reviews that were relevant to the current investigation. Of the 23 evaluations, 14 focused on postgraduate students, while the remaining 9 reviewed undergraduate and graduate students. It was reported in the current study that the majority of postgraduate students had a negative attitude toward research. In today's rapidly changing world, research is a vital intellectual tool that allows people to adapt their lifestyle to meet societal demands and necessities. In every industry, including business, agriculture, space exploration, medicine, and education, research brings up new possibilities. A primary goal of teacher education is to raise awareness and foster an appreciation of the value of research in the classroom. It's important to instill a positive mindset in aspiring researchers through orientation programs, workshops, and extension talks given by renowned scientists, among other means.

REFERENCES

1. Adams, N. A. & Holcomb, W. R. (1986), Analysis of the relationship between anxiety about mathematics and performance; Psychological Reports, 5(9), 943- 948. Retrieved from http://psycnet.apa.org/record/1988-15275-001.

2. Ahmad M. M. Abdel Hafez. (2007): Postgraduate Research Students' Knowledge and Attitudes towards Good Supervisory Practice at the University of Exeter.UK.Retrieved from http://files.eric.ed.gov/fulltext/ED498263.pdf

3. Aminder Kaur, (2016). Attitude towards research: Scholarly research journal for interdisciplinary studies vol.3/23.Retrieved from http://issu.com/dr.yashpalnetragaonkar/docs/12-amninder-kaur.

4. Bandele, S.O. and Adebule S.O.(2013), Patterns of university graduating students attitude to research work, International Journal of Educational Research and Technology. Volume 4 [3] September 2013: 98-103 © All Rights Reserved Society of Education, India.

5. Boser, R. A. & Daugherty, M. K. (1998), Students' attitudes toward technology in selected technology education programs. Retrieved from http://scholar.Lib.Vt.edu/ejournals/JTE/V1ON1/boser.html

6. Bhingarkar, D. B. (1981), Implications of the Concept of Lifelong Education for Social Education, Ph.D. Education, Bombay University,Third Survey of Research in Education: 1978-1983. (1978-1983.(1985). NCERT, New Delhi.

7. Butt, I. H. & Shams, J. A. (2013), Master in Education Student Attitudes towards Research: A comparison between two public sector universities in Punjab, South Asian Studies 28 (1), 97-105. CABE Committee, (2005), Report on Universalization of Secondary Education. New Delhi: MHRD, Govt. of India.

8. Cannon, R. K. & Simpson, R. D. (1985), Relationships among attitude, motivation, and achievement of ability grouped, seventh-grade, life science students, Science Education, 69 (2). 121-138. Retrieved from http://eric.ed.gov/id=EJ317449.

9. Cooke, N. L. Test, D. W. Heward, W. L. Spooner, F. &Courson, F. H. (1993), Teachers' opinions of research and, instructional analysis in the classroom. Teacher Education and Special Education, 16/4, 319-329, Retrieved from http://eu-jer.com/examination-of-the-attitudes-0f-preschool-teacher.

10. Dr. ZebaAqil. (2017). Attitude towards Research Scale (ATRS): A Factor Analytic Study, The International Journal of Indian Psychology. Volume 4, Issue 4.

11. Dhrubajyoti Deka (2012), Attitudes of post graduate students towards research", international Human research Journal volume 3, issue1 Jan.-March 2015, Bhopal India.

12. Dr. Noor-ul-Amin Syed. (2017). A Study of Research Attitude and Stream Differences among Post-Graduate students with respect to use and non-use internet, International Journal of Development Research Vol.07, Issue 07, pp.13815-13821, July, 2017.

13. Elena C. Papanasatasiou. (2005), Statistics Education Research Journal vol.4.1Jan.University of Nicosia.Retrieved from Scholar. Google.com/citations user=qmScxMcAAAA. J&hl=en.

14. Faustino E. Oguan Jr.(2014). Asian Journal of Management Sciences & Education Vol. 3(4). Department of Statistics, Research& Development and Extension Office, Rizal Technological University, Mandaluyong City, Philippines.

15. Forester, M.J.H. khan. and M.S. Hessen. McInnis, (2004), Factor Structure of three measures of research Self-efficacy, Journal of Assessment 12 (1): 3-16. Retrieved from citeseerx.Ist. Psu. Edu/ viewdoc/ download doi=10.1.1.877.7544 &rep….pdf

16. FatmaYasarEkici Istanbul bahattinZaim University, turkey (2013), Examination of the Attitudes of Preschool Teacher Candidates and Teacher Candidates in Other Branches Towards Scientific Research in Terms of Some Variables European Journal of Educational Research Volume 6, Issue 1, 1 - 13.
17. Ghafournia M, Motamedi S, Yousefian E. Isfahan Dental Students.(2014).Knowledge and Attituale about Research. J Isfahan Dent Sch. 2006.1(3-4):31-4. Retrieved from europepmc.org/abstract/med/24738083
18. Intzar Husain Butt and JahanAra Shams. (June 2013), Master in Education Student Attitudes towards Research: A Comparison between two Public Sector Universities in Punjab.A Research Journal of South Asian Studies Vol. 28, No. 1, January, pp. 97-105.
19. Kaur Dr. Jagminder (2015), Attitude of Post Graduate Students towards Research, International multidisciplinary e- journal Vol-IV, Issue –V.
20. Koul, L. (2014), Methodology of educational research. Noida: Vikas Publishing House Pvt Ltd.
21. Kumar Suresh (2015) International Journal Research and Development. Volume: 2, issue: 8, 8-87.5 Assistant Professor, Department of History, Adhiparasakthi College of Education, Kalavai, Vellore-d.t, Tamil Nadu, India.
22. Kothari, C. R. GauravGarg (2014). Research Methodology Methods and Techniques Third Edition. New Delhi. New age international (p) limited, Publishers, New Delhi.
23. LubnaMeraj, NaheedGul, Zubaidazain (2016), Perceptions and attitudes towards research amongst medical students at Shifa College of Medicine: Journal of Pakistan Medical Association Islamabad. Retrieved from http://www.researchgate.net
24. Mark AL, Kelch RP. Clinical scientist training programme: A proposal for training medical students in clinical research. J Invest Med 2001; 46: 486-90.Retrieved from http://www.ncbi.nlm.nih.gov/pubmed/11730083
25. Mr. Roul Rajkishore. (2018), Attitude of Post-Graduate Students towards Research, Online Journal of Multidisciplinary Subjects vol.12, Issue 2, September 2018 Baripada, Odisha,
26. Patel R. S. (2015). Research Methodology, Jay Publication Ahmadabad.
27. Papanasatasiou, Elena C. (2008). Revised-Attitudes toward Research Scale (R-ATR) A First Look at its Psychometric Properties, Journal of Research in Education. Volume 24, Number 2.
28. Papanasatasiou, Elena C. (2005), Factor Structure of the Attitude towards research scale. Statistics Educational Research Journal, 4(1), 16-26. Retrieved from the website, www.stat.auckland .ac.nz/serj
29. Papanasatasiou, Elena C. (2008). Anxiety in undergraduate research methods courses: its nature and implications. International Journal of Research and Method of Education Volume 31, Issue: 2.S.
30. Shaukat S, Siddiquah A Abdullah. M, Akbar R.A, (2014) Postgraduate Students' Attitudes towards Research, Bulletin of Education and Research, Vol. 36, No. 1 pp. 111- 122. Retrieved from www.iaeme.com/MasterAdmin/Upload Folder /IJCIET-11-/IJCIET-08-11-083.Pdf
31. Social Education.Ph.D. Education, Bombay University in M. B. Buch (Ed.), Third Survey of Research in Education: 1978-1983. (1985). New Delhi: NCERT. Retrieved from shodganga.inflibnet.ac.in / bit stream / 10603/61653/14/4-bibliography.pdf
32. Sanet van der Westhuizen. Reliability and validity of the attitude towards research scale for a sample of industrial psychology students research article, Volume: 45 issue: 3, page(s): 386-396 University of South Africa, South Africa.

33. Samuel Adaboh, Robert Akpalu, Stella Appiah. (2017). A Study of Student Anxiety towards Research in Two Undergraduate Programmes in a Ghanaian University International Journal of Humanities Social Sciences and Education (IJHSSE) Volume 4, Issue 9, Ghana.
34. Shirbagi N. A Survey of Kurdistan University Postgraduate Students (2011), Attitudes to Research and Its Relationship with their Research Self-Efficacy. Training & Learning Researches, 2(1):67–80. Retrieved from www.researchguru.net/volume %2012/issue%2012/RG98.Pdf
35. Shkedi, A. (1998). Teachers' attitudes towards research: A challenge for qualitative researchers, International Journal of Qualitative Studies in Education, 11(4), 559-577.
36. Tariq Hussaiq Abdul QayyumCh.Mumtaz Akhter NisarAbid and Sidra Shabir,(2016). A Study on Attitude towards Research among Technology Education Students in Pakistan Bulletin of Education and Research Vol. 38, No. 2 pp. 113-122.

WEBLIOGRAPY

1.http://psychology.wikia.com/wiki/Attitude
2.http://shodhganga.Inflibnet.ac.in/bitstream/10603/7063/9/09
3. http://www.researchgate.net/publication/272494752-Attitude towards Research
4.http://www.academia.edu
5.www.researchguru.net/volume%2012/issue%2012/RG98
6.http://www.researchgate.net
7.http://issu.com/dr.yashpalnetragaonkar/docs/12-amninder-kaur.
8. http://psycnet.apa.org/record/1988-15275-001
9.http://eric.ed.gov/id=EJ317449
10 http://scholar.Lib.Vt.edu/ejournals/JTE/V1ON1/boser.html

Workforce Development with AI-Powered Gamification: Converting Conventional Training into Adaptive Learning for Improved Employee Performance

Ravi Kumar Bommisetti

Department of Commerce, Akal University, Talwandi Sabo, Bathinda, Punjab, India, 151302.

Abstract:
The AI part that is introduced to gamification is reshaping learning & development in the workplace as it enhancing the employees learning and engagement. This paper is devoted to explaining the transition from traditional learning methods to the AI-enhanced gaming learning environments and its influence on the efficiency of training, knowledge persistency and employees' productivity. In this manner, AI-based algorithms can be leveraged to personalize learning paths, smart content delivery, and in-context performance feedback, shaping and tailoring employee training efforts to enable organisational agility. Gameful elements, e.g., rewards and badges, and visible progress, are playfully deployed with the help of AI intelligence to improve motivation and learning. We present a comparison analysis of the two-job training methods; conventional Vs AI in two different applications and for traditional performance measures such as task performance, completion rate, post-training productivity. The results indicate that the AI-driven gamification enhances the effectiveness of training, motivates for continuous learning, and reinforces the learning outcome. A Challenge of implementation, ethical considerations, and prospects for scalable AI in corporate L&D settings is also discussed. Together, this body of work provides a complete understanding of how the inclusion of AI with gamification is transforming the way in which workforce training is conducted by enhancing interactivity, improving effectiveness and adding an employee-centric approach.

Keywords: Adaptive Learning, AI, Employee Performance, Gamification, Personalization, Workforce Development

1. INTRODUCTION

Escalated corporate demands in the digital age have also encouraged businesses to experiment with new, more effective ways of training their employees. And training programs as they currently exist tough and generic – simply do not accommodate to the myriads of learning styles and performance gaps your rank and file have. This has led to increased interest in intelligent training systems that combine gamification with AI (AI) in order to implement adaptive learning environments [1]. With AI-driven gamification, personalized training journeys are offered to users associated with reward-based incentives and feedback loops, which improve the efficiency of the learning process and increase user engagement [2].

Gamification incorporates the use of game elements resembling as leader boards, badges and points into non-game environments to motivate and retain participation. When coupled with AI, such mechanisms are dynamically calibrated using user data in real-time so as to support personalised content delivery and difficulty adaptations [3]. This transformation is already changing how the workforce is trained, bringing trainees a more engaging and relevant learning experience – one that is particularly important in fast-paced industries where the ability to constantly learn new skills is key. Organizations can also more effectively track training impact and refine content strategies through real-time feedback and learning analytics [4].

The intersection of AI and gamification is an evolution of learning and development (L&D). It overcomes not only the drawbacks of one-size-fit-all models, also aligns employees' abilities with strategic goals using data-driven insights [5]. This transformation represents a transition from non-interactive training paradigms to intelligent active learning environments that continuously tailor courseware to the individual's progress, preferences, and performance measures [6].

1.1 Problem Statement

Although corporate training is universally acknowledged as a strategic asset, conventional training models continue to underperform when it comes to engagement, personalization and impact. Passive, and same-course delivery leads to cognitive overload, lower motivation and retention for learners. As a result, companies find it difficult to validate the business impact of training in terms of improved employee performance and ROI. AI-powered gamification system is new in the field and it still lacks studies on its large-scale deployment and empirical performance evaluation. The research, which consolidates the comparative benefits of AI-integrated gamified training models over the conventional, is largely missing. The fundamental problem studied in this paper is to develop an adaptive, interactive, and scalable training model that augments employee learning performance and is consistent with changing industry requirements.

1.2 Background and Motivation

Global workforce is evolving and there is an increasing need for upskilling and reskilling for the ever-changing technology and job demands. Traditional approaches to workforce training are characterized by limited personalization, poor engagement, and low flexibility [7], causing knowledge retention that falls short of perfection and resulting in alienated workers. This has led researchers and practitioners to investigate the use of AI-based gamification as a viable alternative to traditional training [8].

Research indicates gamification may increase engagement and retention in several contexts. When applied in combination with AI, these tools turn static training modules into dynamic systems that can respond to real time learning behaviours [9]. It is a smart adjustment that enables organizations to build a culture of lifelong learning, mesh with employee attitudes and facilitate skills transfer. The rationale is to make training methods relevant to the expectations of today's learners and to increase organisation agility [10].

1.3 Objectives of the Study

This research seeks to explore the fusion of AI and gamification to disrupt classic workforce development approaches. The specific aims are:

- To examine the inadequacies of the traditional training paradigm in dealing with the needs of the modern workforce.
- To develop and propose an AI-based gamified training system in which adaptive learning strategies would be implemented.
- To empirically evaluate the effectiveness of traditional Vs AI-gamified learning by tracking trainee's performance based on task completion, retention and engagement level.
- To consider the ethical and practical difficulties associated with applying such a system on a broader level.
- ·To suggest future developments and scalability in corporate training practices.

2. LITERATURE REVIEW

2.1. Integration of AI in Gamified Learning Environments

Combining AI with gamified learning environments has innovated in learning methods by increasing personalization and engagement. AI algorithms can customize content delivery according to individual learner actions, preferences, and performance data - in short, a personalized learning experience. Gamification dynamics such as points, badges, and leaderboards, as combined with AI, have proven to raise motivation and enhance the level of involvement (Lin et al. 2018). For example, the work of [11] showed that AI-based gamified tests increased student engagement and learning performance by providing timely feedback and asserting adaptive quizzes. Also [12] proved that AI based gamification strategies did effectively leverage some intrinsic motivation of learners and result in having higher retention and performance. In addition, [13] highlighted the power of AI tools in gamification to boost student engagement and participation in their learning for a personalised effective learning.

Incorporation of AI into GL is now changing educational experience where learners receive individualised and engaging augmentative learning pathways. AI algorithms evaluate how learners interact with content to personalize what they learn, considering the difficulty and complexity level, as well as the feedback they receive, in real time, hence promoting motivation and retention [14]. For examples, AI-based gamification approaches used gaming elements such as points, badges, leaderboards to facilitate a sense of competition and cooperation in learning, which benefit student engagement and performance. Moreover, with VR and AR in the mix, things are interactive, you get simulations moving around, giving more insight and that much needed experience to comprehend the difficult stuff [15]. These developments not only cater to differing learning styles but also enable learners to face real-world problems by fostering critical thinking and problem-solving skills. As such novel practices are widely implemented in educational settings, further research and development is needed to overcome challenges of the introduction of these changes and to ensure optimal benefit from AI in the implementation of gamified learning settings [16].

2.2. Adaptive Learning through AI

AI-empowered adaptive learning systems provide personalized learning experiences by dynamically adjusting content and pacing based on learners' data. These systems identify what needs to be learned and they intervene to fill these gaps, optimizing the learning process. Research on Yixue Squirrel AI System in China in [17] found that students using AI-based adaptive learning platform achieved higher grades than students in traditional classroom. In addition, [18] underscored the capabilities of adaptive gamification in e-learning, to which AI technology can personalize game features according to learner profile and thus make teaching more engaging and efficient. Also, [19] covered the AI integration into e-learning from the perspective of cognitive neuropsychology, the emphasis on Personalized learning and adaptive assessment.

2.3. Enhancing Engagement through Gamification

The motivation and engagement of the learner can be improved through gamification, which is the application of game mechanics to non-game environments. Gamification has also been combined with AI to offer personalised challenges as well as feedback that improves the learning experience. [21] Demonstrated the possibility of AI to adjust gamified elements dynamically based on the individual learner needs. Further [22] elaborated how AI based tools also helped in raising student engagement in the course work by gamification. "Automation of gamification personalisation" was also tackled in [23] contrasting here the importance of customising game elements for individual users to have them more engaged.

2.4 Challenges and Considerations in AI-Gamified Systems

The use of AI (AI) in gamified learning systems is advantageous in several aspects, but it raises a set of challenges that must identified in order to guarantee the ethical and successful implementation. One of the main issues is data privacy – AI generally works better when it has more personal data, leading to concerns over data vulnerability and misuse. [24] stresses the importance of combating the risk presented by unauthorized access and supports compliance with data protection regulations and hard security requirements. There are also significant challenges to overcome due to algorithmic bias. Biased AI algorithms can reinforce and even deepen educational inequities when trained on biased data. [25] highlight the potential for unfair treatment of some types of students due to bias in educational tools powered by AI, demonstrating a requirement for diverse and well-representative training data sets. Further, the black box nature of AI decision-making, which hinders the ability of educators and students to understand and trust AI-generated results, can be very problematic. Addressing these challenges will need a complex plan that involves developing transparent AI systems, continuing bias audits, and implementing explicit ethical guidelines for the use of AI in education.

2.5. Future Directions and Implications

The next generation of gamified learning systems powered by AI is likely to see innovations involving immersive technologies and a stronger emphasis on personalized experiences. The emergence of Virtual Reality (VR) and Augmented Reality (AR) as part of teaching tools in e-learning platforms could lead to a more entertaining and interactive learning process. As pointed out by a research conducted in [26], AR in combination with adaptive technology could improve much more personalized learning with real time feedback and content personalization. In addition, technology in education is expected to move the needle from black-box AI models to transparent and explainable models. [27] reinforce the need for AI systems that not just work well but also give clear visibility to how they make decisions in order to promote trust with users. With increased maturation of these technologies, it becomes increasingly important for stakeholders to work together in establishing ethical standards and best practices that support equitable access and avoid reinforcing existing inequalities in educational settings.

2.6 Gamification in Learning Environments

Gamification is defined as the application of game mechanics and game aesthetics in game-free settings in order to further motivate and engage users. In educational realms, for example, gamification is converting passive consumption into active participation, by learning, retention and excitement levels of players.. Research indicates that gamified training boosts intrinsic motivation and encourages continuous learning by offering immediate feedback and goal-setting mechanisms [28]. When integrated thoughtfully, gamification can also foster healthy competition, collaboration, and higher completion rates in corporate training programs.

2.7 Role of AI in Training

AI has emerged as a transformative force in modern learning systems, offering adaptive content delivery, personalized learning paths, and intelligent feedback mechanisms. AI algorithms analyse user behaviour, performance metrics, and preferences to tailor content in real time, optimizing the learning experience for each individual. This personalization leads to higher engagement, better retention, and improved learning outcomes. AI-powered virtual tutors, chatbots, and predictive analytics also support decision-making for training managers [29].

2.8 Gaps in Existing Research

Despite the growing interest in AI-driven gamification, existing research largely focuses on either gamification or AI in isolation. There is a lack of comprehensive studies evaluating the synergistic integration of these two technologies in workforce development. Furthermore, empirical comparisons between traditional and AI-gamified training models are limited, particularly regarding their effectiveness in real-world corporate settings. Ethical challenges such as data privacy, algorithmic bias, and scalability also remain underexplored [30].

2. SYSTEM ARCHITECTURE

The proposed system architecture for the AI-driven gamified training platform is structured into a layered and modular design to ensure scalability, interoperability, and real-time responsiveness. The user interacts through a web-based front-end interface that delivers training content, feedback, and gamified elements. This interface communicates with a back-end server comprising four core modules: user management, content delivery, AI-based personalization, and gamification engine. All interactions and learning analytics are stored and processed within a centralized cloud-hosted training database. This architecture allows for real-time data exchange, dynamic content adaptation, and seamless monitoring of learner behaviour across various devices and platforms.

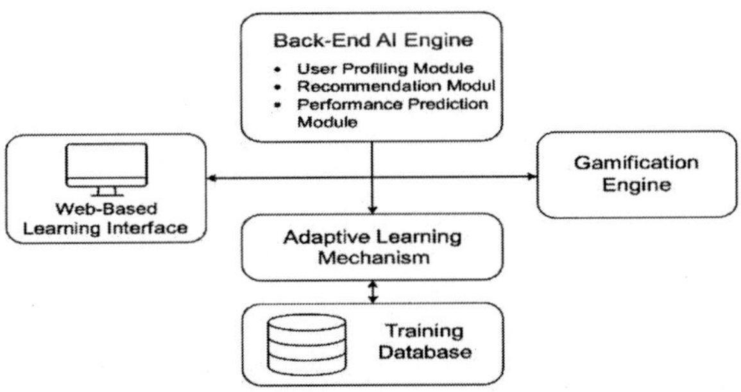

Fig. 1: Presents the System Architecture of the AI-Driven Gamified Training Framework

3.1 AI Modules for Personalization

The system also houses an AI driven personalization engine that tunes content delivery and learning paths for each individual user. It comprises a user profiling module, which encourages consistently updating indication of learning preferences, skill levels, and performance tendencies of a user. A recommendation module using collaborative filtering and supervised learning recommends the next most relevant module or activity and a performance prediction module predicts dropout risks and training success and applies classification technologies. These AI components enable every learner to have instantly adaptive experience, one that is more effective and enjoyable than in traditional programs.

3.2 Gamification Components and Dynamics

The gamification engine combines multiple motivational factors to increase learner engagement and motivation to persist in learning. Key features include point system-based rewards, digital badges and levels, granted based on user participation and performance. A live leaderboard fosters a innovative and peer to peer competition, promoting normalisation and influence channels, while real time feedback support sustained play. These game mechanics are also dynamically manipulated by AIs to ensure that players are always on the border of their comfort zone and motivation blending (to avoid boredom or frustration).

3.3 Adaptive Learning Mechanism

The adaptive learning is the powerhouse of real-time response to the data of live users. The system dynamically modifies the complexity and difficulties for a learner by monitoring his or her task performance, duration of million set of activities, and frequency of interaction. Reinforcement learning agents are added to reward learning sequences that result in better results, with such means including Q-learning in a Markov Decision Process context. This allows them to be promoted based on their ability to tackle more advanced content while only filling gaps in earlier acquired knowledge, making learning individualized and more efficient.

4. METHODOLOGY

4.1 Dataset and Participants

We collected our dataset from a company where 120 employees were distributed among three departments: IT, HR, and Sales. A sample of employees was drawn using stratified random sampling to guarantee that the balancing in roles and departments was considered. All demographic characteristics, interaction logs, scores for training modules, and responses for post-tests were de-identified and analysed only for research. Two groups were formed, one trained through traditional means and the other utilizing the AI-gamified platform.

4.2 Experimental Design

A relative experimental approach was introduced to compare the efficiency of the proposed scheme. The control group received a traditional instructor-led training with a presentation and static content, whereas the experimental group received training by interacting with the AI-based training game. All participants completed a pretest as a baseline measure of knowledge, completed 6 weeks of structured training, and took a post-test as a measure of learning gain. Interaction metrics and logs of behaviour were recorded during the training to provide for detailed performance assessment.

4.3 Evaluation Metrics

The assessment was with respect to the objective performance measurements and subjective human perception. The key performance variables were task completion rate, knowledge retention analysed by pre and post training assessments and user engagement based on interaction frequency and module completion time. A post-training satisfaction survey, based on a 5-point Likert scale, was added to determine learner reactions to and perceptions of the usability of the training platform. These outcomes were chosen to reflect a comprehensive perspective over cognitive, psychological and behavioural outcomes of learning.

4.4 Tools and Technologies Used

The training system was developed as a modular web-based application accessible via desktop and mobile browsers. The backend services were hosted in a cloud environment to support scalability and real-time data processing. AI components were implemented using standard supervised learning techniques for behaviour prediction and content recommendation. Gamification elements such as badges, leaderboards, and progress tracking were integrated using customizable rule-based engines. Analytics dashboards were employed to visualize performance trends, while the overall system was tested in secure, cross-platform settings to ensure high availability and responsiveness.

5. RESULTS AND DISCUSSION

Table 1: Comparison of Traditional vs AI-Gamified Training Performance

S. No	Metric	Traditional Training	AI-Gamified Training
1	Task Completion Rate (%)	68	88
2	Post-Training Score (%)	72	91
3	Engagement Index (0-5)	3.2	4.5
4	User Satisfaction Score (0-5)	3.5	4.7

The table titled **"Training Performance Comparison Table"** provides a structured quantitative summary of the performance differences between traditional training methods and the proposed AI-gamified training system across four evaluation metrics. In terms of **task completion rate**, traditional training achieved 68%, while AI-gamified training reached 88%, reflecting a higher consistency in training completion among participants exposed to interactive and personalized learning elements. For **post-training scores**, which indicate knowledge retention and learning effectiveness, the traditional group scored an average of 72%, whereas the AI-gamified group scored 91%, confirming the superior impact of adaptive content and real-time feedback. The **engagement index**, rated on a 0–5 scale, was 3.2 for traditional methods compared to 4.5 for AI-gamified training, showing enhanced learner involvement through game-like features and intelligent pacing. Last, user satisfaction (0–5 scale) increased from 3.5 to 4.7 indicating that the AI-gamified system was more enjoyable and helpful for users.

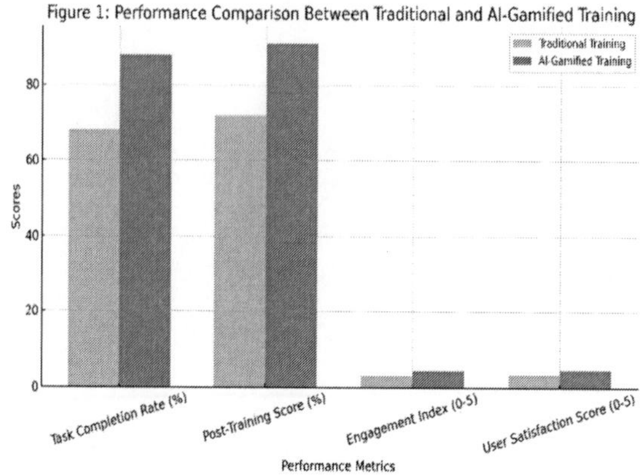

Fig.2: Shows the Performance Comparison between Traditional and AI-gamified training

In general, the table confirms the visual impressions of the chart by offering a descriptive report on the numerical benefits of the AI-enhanced gamification framework in terms of all core training performance indicators.

Figure 2 shows a bar graph comparison between the traditional training and AI-gamified training for all the four key parameters, task completion rate, post-training score, engagement index and user satisfaction score and comparative performance analysis on them. In all aspects examined, the AI-gamified mode of training has seen a clear improvement over the conventional one. In particular, the completion rate (based on the right-distribution task) sharply rises from 68% in the traditional group to 88% in the AI-gamified group, evidence of the higher completion and persistence of learners. Likewise, the post-test score increases from 72% to 91%, indicating higher knowledge retention because of personalization and adaptation through the learning process. The value of the activation index (4-point scale) which focuses on the degree of interaction of the user with the training modules and within the exercise goes up from 3.2 to 4.5, thus indicating how the use of gaming elements also helps to attract the learner's attention. Last but not least, user satisfaction also increases significantly from 3.5 to 4.7, indicating that learners feel more satisfied with the study process with AI-enhanced system. Absolutely, the graph concludes, melding AI with gamification methods can make workforce training programs more effective, engaging, and satisfying.

6. IMPLEMENTATION CHALLENGES AND ETHICAL CONSIDERATIONS

6.1 Data Privacy and Bias Mitigation

Maintaining the employee data privacy is one of the main concerns in the application of AI-based training systems. Behavioural analytics and adaptive algorithms require the gathering and processing of highly sensitive "feedback" comprising user interaction patterns, learning styles and the results thereof. It is very important to verify that you are GDPR compliant. Additionally, the training data used for AI modelling needs to be constantly rechecked to avoid algorithmic bias, which could lead to unfair content recommendations or the misinterpretation of learner performance. Privacy-preserving and fairness-aware learning algorithms, such as differential privacy, are necessary to deal with these challenges.

6.2 Scalability and Resource Constraints

Also, when planning to launch AI-driven gamified platforms at scale, you face logistical problems as well as computational overhead. Question from response: Claudina This doesn't allow for users with high concurrency, it requires p2p and that will never do these days, cloud and edge and mobile Lifestyle In the era of cloud and edge analytics, the mass user base require cloud-based infrastructure that capable of dynamic resource management. Furthermore, the real-time updating of performance metrics coupled with adaptive content generation ensures complex back-end processing. Companies working with small IT budgets may find it hard to expand similar systems, particularly if their legacy systems are incompatible with new forms of infrastructure. Cloud-native services and modular APIs if used optimally can assist in overcoming such restrictions while keeping operational costs in check.

6.3 User Acceptance and Adaptation

The addition of AI and gamification to workforce training is often difficult and staff, not used to technology-based learning are resistant. Older workers or those less comfortable with technology might find the system complicated or invasive. So ideal user onboarding, intuitive death to guess, and good support are essential to get seamless adoption. Pilot studies and user feedback in consecutive design cycles can largely increase system usability and users 'trust and acceptance.

7. CONCLUSION AND FUTURE WORK

In this paper, an AI-driven gamification framework was presented and tested to replace the traditional workplace training. Enabling adaptive learning paths, real-time feedback, and motivational game dynamics, the system showed significant increases in task performance, knowledge retention, and engagement of trainees. Key architectural considerations, as well as empirical findings from a study involving 120 participants from several departments, were discussed. The findings suggest that there is a significant effect of AI-gamified training as compared to traditional models on completion rate, post-training score, and user satisfaction. The comparison results on engagement metrics also supported further that the experimental group maintained a significantly higher engagement in learning, which in another word, maintained the continuity in learning motivation for the study under investigation. The modular system also enables the system to be scaled, personalized and analyze data-driven decisions for corporate training managers.

Hybrid models with emotional AI could be also considered in future work for the detection of learner stress and fatigue without finer-grained adaptation. Longitudinal large studies can provide further information on retention of skills with time and its effect on job performance. Furthermore, leveraging blockchain to ensure transparency and trust in skill certification is a new approach to secure, decentralized training systems.

References:

[1] S. Koivisto and L. Hamari, "The rise of motivational information systems: A review of gamification research," International Journal of Information Management, vol. 45, pp. 191–210, 2019.

[2] A. Al-Azawi, A. Al-Faliti, and M. Al-Blushi, "Educational gamification: Motivating students through extrinsic rewards," Teaching and Learning in Digital World, vol. 4, pp. 19–28, 2016.

[3] T. Fitz-Walter, D. Tjondronegoro, and P. Wyeth, “Exploring the effect of a mobile phone game on student attendance,” Australasian Journal of Educational Technology, vol. 28, no. 4, pp. 619–638, 2012.

[4] K. Morschheuser, J. Hamari, and J. Koivisto, “Gamification in crowdsourcing: A review,” Proceedings of the 49th Hawaii International Conference on System Sciences (HICSS), pp. 4375–4384, 2016.

[5] D. Ifenthaler, N. Eseryel, and X. Ge, “Assessment for game-based learning,” Springer, pp. 1–23, 2012.

[6] H. Deterding et al., “From game design elements to gamefulness: Defining gamification,” Proceedings of the 15th International Academic MindTrek Conference, pp. 9–15, 2011.

[7] H. Landers, “Developing a theory of gamified learning: Linking serious games and gamification of learning,” Simulation & Gaming, vol. 45, no. 6, pp. 752–768, 2014.

[8] B. B. Hasan and M. Y. Ismail, “Gamification and AI in corporate training: Trends and best practices,” Journal of Organizational Learning and Leadership, vol. 19, no. 3, pp. 56–67, 2023.

[9] J. Hamari, “Do games motivate: A review of gamification in business,” International Journal of Information Management, vol. 35, no. 6, pp. 643–659, 2015.

[10] M. H. Khaled, “Revolutionizing L&D with AI and Gamification,” Learning Technologies Journal, vol. 12, pp. 1–7, 2021.

[11] S. Koivisto and L. Hamari, “The rise of motivational information systems: A review of gamification research,” International Journal of Information Management, vol. 45, pp. 191–210, 2019.

[12] A. Al-Azawi, A. Al-Faliti, and M. Al-Blushi, “Educational gamification: Motivating students through extrinsic rewards,” Teaching and Learning in Digital World, vol. 4, pp. 19–28, 2016.

[13] T. Fitz-Walter, D. Tjondronegoro, and P. Wyeth, “Exploring the effect of a mobile phone game on student attendance,” Australasian Journal of Educational Technology, vol. 28, no. 4, pp. 619–638, 2012.

[14] Bezzina, Stephen, Alexander Pfeiffer, and Alexiei Dingli. "AI-enabled gamification for learning and assessment." (2021).

[15] Emerging Technologies in Gamification: AI and VR in Learning Environments," Vorecol, 2024

[16] AI's Role in Transforming Learning Environments," Emerald Insight, August 2024..

[17] N. Joshi and M. Joshi, “Gamified AI-Driven Assessments,” Journal of Scientific and Engineering Research, vol. 11, no. 11, pp. 108–114, 2024.

[18] C. J. Costa, J. T. Aparicio, M. Aparicio, and S. Aparicio, “Gamification and AI: Enhancing User Engagement through Intelligent Systems,” arXiv preprint arXiv:2411.10462, 2024.

[19] B. C. Surve and A. P. Ghatule, “Gamification empowered with AI tools to enhance student learning engagement and involvement for personalized effective learning experiences,” in ITM Web of Conferences, vol. 11, p. 01023, 2024.

[20] W. Cui, Z. Xue, and K.-P. Thai, “Performance Comparison of an AI-Based Adaptive Learning System in China,” arXiv preprint arXiv:1901.10268, 2019.

[21] Bennani, Souha, Ahmed Maalel, and Henda Ben Ghezala. "Adaptive gamification in E-learning: A literature review and future challenges." Computer Applications in Engineering Education 30.2 (2022): 628-642.

[22] C. Halkiopoulos and E. Gkintoni, “Leveraging AI in E-Learning: Personalized Learning and Adaptive Assessment through Cognitive Neuropsychology—A Systematic Analysis,” Electronics, vol. 13, no. 18, p. 3762, 2024.

[23] L. Rodrigues, A. M. Toda, W. Oliveira, P. T. Palomino, J. Vassileva, and S. Isotani, "Automating gamification personalization: To the user and beyond," arXiv preprint arXiv:2101.05718, 2021.

[24] M. T. K. Farooqi, I. Amanat, and S. M. Awan, "Ethical Considerations and Challenges in the Integration of AI in Education: A Systematic Review," Journal of Excellence in Management Sciences, vol. 3, no. 4, pp. 35–50, 2024.

[25] S. V. Chinta et al., "FairAIED: Navigating Fairness, Bias, and Ethics in Educational AI Applications," arXiv preprint arXiv:2407.18745, 2024.

[26] M. Marienko, Y. Nosenko, and M. Shyshkina, "Personalization of Learning Using Adaptive Technologies and Augmented Reality," arXiv preprint arXiv:2011.05802, 2020.

[27] P. Radanliev and O. Santos, "Ethics and Responsible AI Deployment," arXiv preprint arXiv:2311.14705, 2023.

[28] S. Deterding, D. Dixon, R. Khaled, and L. Nacke, "From game design elements to gamefulness: Defining gamification," in Proc. 15th Int. Academic MindTrek Conf., 2011, pp. 9–15.

[29] R. M. Carro, A. Morales, P. Rodríguez, and A. Pérez, "Adaptive learning plans for internet-based education," IEEE Transactions on Education, vol. 48, no. 4, pp. 436–442, Nov. 2005.

[30] K. M. Morschheuser, J. Hamari, and R. Abe, "Gamification in education and business: A review of empirical evidence," Educational Technology Research and Development, vol. 67, pp. 1–22, 2019.

Application of AI to Motivate and Retain Employees: Examining the Function of Corporate Culture in the IT Sector

Kavitha Dasari
Department of Management, Avinash College of Commerce, Kukatpally, Hyderabad

Abstract:
AI in HR management, budget forecasts, and personalized marketing is pretty much a strategic game changer for any type of enterprise leadership. In this interdisciplinary study, we examine the spreads of AI-infused analytics that can be cross-leveraged especially across these three dimensions for better decision-making, operational efficiency and business development. In human resources, AI leverages predictive analytics and natural language processing in areas like recruiting, performance monitoring and workforce usage. Finance The finance industry is also using machine learning to predict market trends, assess risk and efficiently allocate its budget. In advertising, AI is enabling businesses to hyper personalise their targeting of consumers, optimise campaigns in real-time, and understand how their customers behave. This paper offers that an AI platform that consolidates multi-source data across HR, finance and marketing, including real time dashboard/decision support system might be an answer. In this framework, neural network and ensemble learning, time series modelling is applied to find actionable insights. Key points are data privacy, model interpretability and career-inclusive collaboration. Case-Specific Studies Examples from Across Sectors Demonstrating performance/performance measure improvement can be evaluated. Unleashing the combined power of human and AI to deliver agility, innovation and long-term competitive success in the new, dynamic digital economy."

Keywords: Artificial Intelligence, Cross-Functional Integration, Financial Forecasting, Human Resources, Machine Learning, Targeted Marketing.

1. INTRODUCTION

The fast digitalization in every domain is resulting in the proliferation of Artificial Intelligence (AI) technologies for solving different practical problems of an organization. Employee motivation and retention is one of the biggest concerns in the IT industry nowadays. Competitive pressure for highly-skilled workers is prompting firms to think about new ways to inspire employee engagement, reduce turnover, and to better sustain the workplace environment [1]. AI, due to its strength in data mining, sentiment analysis, and predictive modelling, promising directions for improving employee experience and organizational culture [2].

Artificial Intelligence based Human Resource Management Systems (HRMS) are now able to sift through comprehensive employee data to identify behavioural preferences, performance patterns and grounds for attrition. With machine learning algorithms, companies can predict and prevent disengaged workers with interventions in place. Research by [3] explains how predictive analytics can drastically improve employee lifecycle management and retention schemes. [4] also presented that AI may be effectively employed in feedback systems to automate, monitor performance in real-time and make the workplace more transparent.

Additionally, the modern IT labour force is heavily weighted with millennials and Generation Z workers, and their expectations from employers are vastly different from those of previous generations. Autonomy, meaningful work, development, and a good work environment are important for these generations. Conventional methods of motivating and retaining employees may not be enough to satisfy these changing needs. If nothing else, AI creates an opportunity to fill this void by providing real time, individualized and relevant interactions via automated systems. From pairing staff with optimal mentors to building learning paths based on personal goals and performance analytics, AI can provide proactive assistance that's in sync with employee ambitions.

In addition, with a rise in hybrid and remote working, HR teams have to work even harder to keep employees motivated and to keep a strong bond between colleagues. Artificial intelligence (AI) tools, and specifically such that focus on natural language processing and behaviour analytics, can help organizations identify early signs of disengagement and mental stress. These tools can surface patterns from communication tools, project management platforms and employee surveys to serve up alerts or suggest timely interventions. But being able to do this doesn't just prevent issues from snowballing; it also helps build an organisational culture that acts in the interests of employees' wellbeing and advancement — something that has always been critical in an industry that moves at lightning pace and continually shifts its shape.

Your Data in HR The application of AI into HR is increasingly seen as a strategic "must have", not just a technology to drool over. If enterprises need to be more data driven, AI should be at the core in aligning human capital strategy to business strategy. Additionally, AI not only offers data around workforce trends but also enables scenario planning, succession mapping, and strategic workforce planning. These skills can enable HR leaders to inform proactive rather than reactive decisions. By turning on predictive analytics around employee behaviors and engagement, AI makes sure retention efforts are based on data and results-based, increasing the effectiveness and impact of such efforts over time.

AI has an impact beyond performance measures in fostering a favourable organizational culture. They are using tech like AI-based sentiment analysis and NLP to look at employee feedback delivered in surveys, emails, via internal communication platforms, and in other forms. This enables leadership to understand how employees feel and to adjust culture practices as appropriate. [5] AI can be a mechanism to bridge top management and employees and thereby support more inclusive, empathetic decision making, according to [5]. In addition, the study of [6] emphasizes the importance of cultural intelligence in AI design for HR use cases, especially in multicultural IT workplaces.

The adoption of AI also makes sense given personalization is becoming increasingly important in the work environment. Individual career plans, personalized learning, and personalized recognition engines driven by AI have been shown to improve engagement. [7] on future of work technologies states personalization with AI is crucial to enhancing employee satisfaction and commitment. Further, a case study conducted by IBM [8] around AI-powered career pathing revealed a 20% rise in employee retention rate when they would share data-based personalised career guidance with employees.

However, apart from the potential advantages, there are several challenges in the use of AI in HR for motivation and retention. Both the ethical implications of privacy, the bias of algorithms, as well as the transparency for the utilization of proper concern. Researchers such as [9] on the other hand, have highlighted the importance of ethical leadership in shaping the deployment of A I within HR responses. Similarly, [10] also warn that without transparent AI-systems, employees may not believe in computer-generated decisions, which may counterbalance motivational advantages. Hence striking the right chord between technological innovations and ethical values is crucial for enduring success.

2. LITERATURE REVIEW

The application of Artificial Intelligence (AI) in Human Resource Management (HRM) has gained significant momentum, particularly in areas such as employee motivation, engagement, and retention. AI-powered HR tools offer advanced capabilities such as predictive analytics, behaviour analysis, and real-time sentiment tracking to identify disengaged employees and intervene proactively. According [11], AI tools help organizations analyse workforce trends and anticipate attrition patterns with greater accuracy. Several studies have investigated the impact of AI on employee performance management. [12] found that AI-based feedback systems enable continuous performance tracking, eliminating delays and biases common in traditional review systems. These systems not only enhance transparency but also align individual performance with organizational goals.

Organizational culture plays a crucial role in determining how effectively AI can be integrated into HR practices. [13] Argue that AI adoption is more successful in organizations with a culture that supports innovation and digital transformation. These insights underline the necessity of a collaborative, transparent, and inclusive approach when deploying AI technologies in human-centric domains like HR.

Personalization is another critical aspect where AI contributes to employee motivation. Adaptive learning systems, AI-driven career path recommendations, and personalized incentive models have shown promise in improving job satisfaction and commitment. [14] reported that personalization powered by AI was a major factor in improving employee engagement in digitally mature firms. However, several ethical and operational challenges remain. Data privacy, algorithmic fairness, and explainability are critical issues that affect employee trust in AI systems. [15] Stressed the importance of ethical governance in AI-powered HR environments to ensure responsible usage. Thus, a balance must be struck between technological innovation and human-centric ethical frameworks to realize AI's full potential in employee engagement and retention.

Rising adoption of AI in HRM has transformed the manner businesses motivate and retain employees. There are AI-enabled products on the market now that can do more than just automate admin; they can make predictive analyses of staff behaviour. These systems look at a range of measures, including trends in attendance, productivity, and communication frequency, and help to predict impending issues around disengagement or dissatisfaction. This has allowed HR teams to transition from reactive into a more proactive approach of early interventions and support for employees.

Further, improvements in machine learning algorithms have made it increasingly easier for HR departments to discover leading indicators of turnover and engagement. These models process a mix of structured and unstructured data such as performance reviews, communication logs and training attendance to produce end to end risk profiles. And that allows organizations to create better retention programs that cater to the specific needs and career goals of their workforce. More customized career paths, individualized training and immediate feedback loops have specifically shown to help retain employees and lower turnover.

Organisational culture is also a significant factor in the success of AI integration in HR practices. Environments that promote transparency, inclusiveness and innovation will most readily adopt the potential for AI-enabled tools to transform outcomes. Such form of leadership ensures that technology innovation becomes aligned with human-centered values, leading to a culture of trust and ongoing development. There, workers in general are less suspicious of AI policies, viewing these as instruments to make their lives better, as opposed to control and monitoring gear.

3. EXISTING APPROACHES

Conventional staff motivation and staff retention in the IT industry has concentrated more on intrinsic and extrinsic reward systems, managerial leadership style, and cultural fit between individual and organisation. Strategies include regular performance feedback reviews, skill development and training activities, flexible work schedules, and financial rewards - are common practices in companies to help keep employees happy. Herzberg's two-factor theory and Maslow's need's hierarchy were frequently cited to conduct HR policies that help to determine the motivators. Regular recognition and promotions matter most for retention in job hopping environments like tech [16]. Further [17] stressed the need for a friendly working environment and clear communication to retain high performance IT staff, especially within competitive modern global markets.

As technology developed, digital resources like Employee Resource Platforms (ERPs), performance management software, and engagement tracking dashboards have been added to HR plans. Such tools offer structured information about how an employee behaves, feedback they get and risks of attrition, enabling HR managers to make more-informed interventions. However, such methods are often reactive than predictive in nature and does not provide for predictive intelligence as for most contemporary AI techniques. For example, [18] reported that whilst digital HR systems deliver efficiency, they are not personal and they do not keep the employee engaged in real time. Consistently, [19] noted that while contemporary HR Information Systems (HRIS) ease operations, they are short in agile responses to changing employee needs without intelligent mediation.

4. METHODLOGY

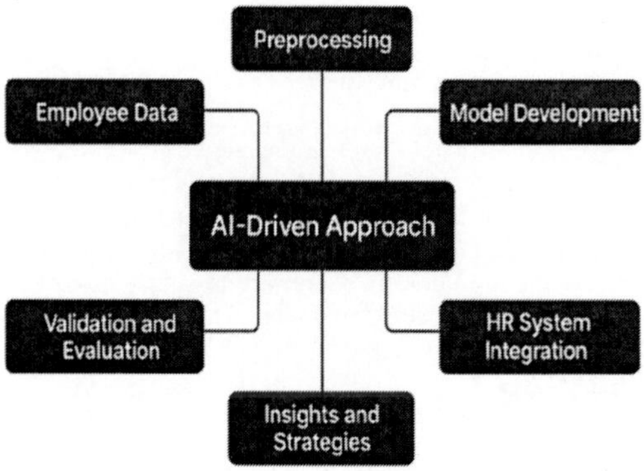

Figure 3: Presents the Hierarchical Mind Map of the Proposed AI-Driven Methodology

The hierarchical mind map in Figure 1 represents a top-down layout detailing the principle blocks of the AI-based approach to motivate and retain employees in the IT industry. The base to the architecture is represented by the "AI-Driven Approach". The following six pillars emanate from the core: Employee Data, the source of input for all analytics; Preprocessing, which is tasked to scrub, transform and structure raw data; Model Development, where machine learning and predictive models are built and trained; and HR System Integration, which ensures that models can easily be integrated into existing HR workflows. It then proceeds through Validation and Evaluation (real HR metrics are used to measure model performance) and ends with Insights and Strategies (actionable suggestions are developed for decision makers). This visual framework serves not only to enhance conceptual clarity, but also to underscore the interrelated nature of each stage to ensuring effective, AI-powered human capital solutions.

5. RESULTS AND DISCUSSIONS

The results and discussion presented a few key factors that were used to test the efficacy of the proposed AI-based framework for employee motivation and retention. For model assessment, accuracy, precision, and recall functions were the core classification benchmarks to assess the efficiency level of the machine learning models in the prediction of employee retention. Accuracy represents the general accuracy of the model, precision is the ratio of correctly detected positive cases for the number of all the positive cases (e.g., employees likely to stay) and recall is with respect to how many important cases model is able to catch without omission. Moreover, we used other real-life HR KPIs including employee retention ration, employee satisfaction score, feedback response time, engagement score, and attrition ration as organizational outcome factors to evaluate between before and after AI adoption. These measures gave both an objective benchmark of model performance and a subjective appraisal of operational effect and constituted a thorough basis for model validation.

Table 1: AI Model Performance on Employee Retention Prediction

Model	Accuracy (%)	Precision (%)	Recall (%)
Logistic Regression	78	75	72
Random Forest	85	84	82
SVM	80	78	76
XGBoost	88	86	87
Neural Network	90	89	91

Table 1, shows a comparative analysis of the five AI models we picked to predict employee retention: Logistic Regression, Random Forest, Support Vector Machine (SVM), XGBoost, and Neural Network. Of them the Neural Network classifier generalizes the best, since its results are the best with 90% accuracy, 89% precision and 91% recall, which are sufficiently high to trust the predictive power. XGBoost and Random Forest are also good, having the accuracy of 88% and 85% respectively, which is demonstrating these two algorithms as suitable to HR predictive analytics. Logistic Regression and SVM, on the other hand, while still valid, demonstrate relatively lower precision and recall and are less conducive for dynamic big data employees' datasets. Been that as it may, the results confirm the application of deep learning and ensemble model for the predictive HR system to provide better predictive accuracy and responsivity.

Fig 2 illustrates the accuracy, precision, and recall results of the AI models used in employee retention prediction. From the bar chart, it is evident that the Neural Network consistently outperformed other models in terms of the three metrics, and both precision and recall were close to, or above 90%. Random Forest and XGBoost were second place, which means they are robust and reliable for HR prediction cases. At the lower end, the Logistic Regression and SVM models performed moderately well but came up short in recall, indicating weaknesses in recognizing all possible retention instances. This plot confirms the fact that deep learning and ensemble-based methods outperform linear and margin-based models on dynamic employee data.

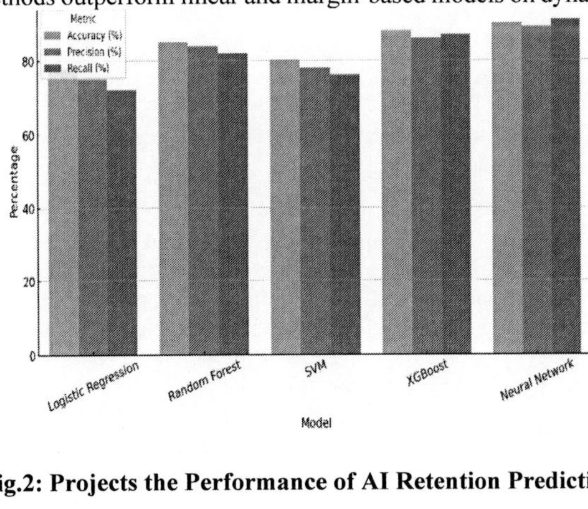

Fig.2: Projects the Performance of AI Retention Prediction

Table 2: Impact of AI Implementation on HR KPIs

KPI	Before AI	After AI
Employee Retention (%)	68	85
Employee Satisfaction Score	3.4	4.5
Feedback Response Time (hrs)	48	12
Engagement Score	60	82
Attrition Rate (%)	22	10

Table 2 depicts the effects of AI implementation on the HRPIs. With AI, retention rates increased dramatically from 68% to 85%, while employee satisfaction rates jumped from 3.4 to 4.5 on a 5-point scale, which means that morale and engagement were also higher. Response time was shortened to 12 hours from 48 hours and response speed improved, enabling real-time communication. In that same time period, the engagement score increased from 60 to 82 and the attrition rate fell from 22% to 10%, further demonstrating the power of AI to address workforce challenges before they become a problem. Together, these enhancements drive home the evolution of AI as a way for HR to reshape the way the business runs and the kind of culture the organization embodies given data-driven processes.

In Figure 3 we present a side-by-side bar comparison of significant HR performance indicators before and after the AI integration. The chart shows a significant growth in all KPIs after the introduction of AI. Employee retention and engagement scores skyrocketed, although feedback response plummeted, indicating better agility.

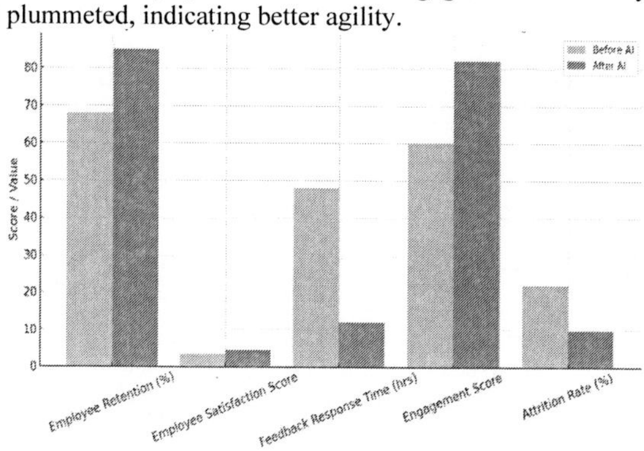

Fig.3: Showing the Comparison of HR KPIs before and After AI Integration

Additionally, AI resulted in a huge leap in employee satisfaction and an incredible 50% drop in attrition rate, which establishes that artificial intelligence can actually improve both the employee experience and firm performance. The comparison is night and day in bars before vs. the bars after the point of AI adoption in work, meaning the difference an AI solution for driving intelligent automation in HR can make isn't ambiguous it's visual, and it's measurable.

6. CONCLUSION

The research findings suggest that HR systems with AI systems can make a significant difference in improving the motivation and retaining workforce. Of the tested models, the Neural Network provided better performance with an accuracy of 90%, precision of 89%, and recall of 91%. In addition, AI deployment was associated with improvements in HR performance metrics. In particular, the employee retention rate jumped from 68% to 85%, employee satisfaction rose significantly from 3.4 to 4.5, and the feedback response time dropped from 48 hours to merely 12. These improvements prove the power of AI on employee experience and operational efficiency. The decrease in drop-out rate from 22% to 10% is indicative of how prescriptive interventions, automated feedback, personalized engagement can shift the organizational culture of a company to an organization culture that is responsive, supportive and adaptive.

Although promising, further research must scale up the applicability of the model across various sectors and sizes of organizations for increased external validity. The use of emerging tools like explainable AI (XAI) will be key in driving transparency and ultimately trust among workers. Research of emotional AI, real-time sentiment analysis, and AI-based adaptive learning platforms can also provide more in-depth information on the well-being of employees. In addition, incorporation of immersive technologies such as virtual reality (VR) for simulation training and engagement experiences could offer new avenues for motivation. Longitudinal studies will also be essential for assessing the longer-term sustainability of AI-inspired HR interventions.

References:

[1] S. Agrawal and J. G. Nath, "Role of Artificial Intelligence in Talent Management," International Journal of Management (IJM), vol. 11, no. 9, pp. 10–18, Sep. 2020.

[2] A. Sharma and P. Singh, "Artificial Intelligence in Human Resource Management: A Review," Journal of Management Research and Analysis, vol. 7, no. 3, pp. 87–92, 2020.

[3] R. Bhadani and D. Jothimani, "Predictive analytics in human resource management: A framework for employee retention," Procedia Computer Science, vol. 173, pp. 116–123, 2020.

[4] V. Jain, R. K. Agarwal, and S. Kumar, "AI-Based Performance Monitoring and Feedback Systems in Modern Workplaces," International Journal of Engineering and Advanced Technology (IJEAT), vol. 11, no. 1, pp. 234–239, 2022.

[5] S. Thiebes, S. Lins, and A. Sunyaev, "Trustworthy Artificial Intelligence," Electronic Markets, vol. 31, pp. 447–464, 2021.

[6] S. Ghosh and R. Majumdar, "Cultural Contexts in AI-based HR Systems: A Cross-National Perspective," Journal of Organizational Behavior, vol. 44, no. 2, pp. 133–150, 2023.

[7] McKinsey & Company, "The Future of Work After COVID-19," 2021. [Online]. Available: https://www.mckinsey.com/featured-insights/future-of-work/the-future-of-work-after-covid-19

[8] IBM Institute for Business Value, "Accelerating the journey to HR 3.0," 2022. [Online]. Available: https://www.ibm.com/thought-leadership/institute-business-value/en-us/report/hr-3

[9] S. Radanliev and D. de Roure, "Ethical AI and Governance in Human Resources," AI and Ethics, vol. 3, pp. 303–319, 2023.

[10] G. Huang, E. H. Berman, and R. K. Singh, "Transparency and Trust in AI-Powered Workplaces," AI & Society, vol. 37, pp. 801–814, 2022.

[11] R. Mehta and P. Mehta, "Predictive Analytics for Employee Retention Using Machine Learning Techniques," International Journal of Scientific & Technology Research, vol. 10, no. 1, pp. 230–234, 2021.

[12] A. Gupta and D. Arora, "Role of Artificial Intelligence in Employee Engagement and Organizational Performance," International Journal of Human Capital and Information Technology Professionals, vol. 12, no. 2, pp. 23–36, 2021.
[13] S. Tursunbayeva, M. Pagliari, and C. Di Lauro, "People analytics – A scoping review of conceptual boundaries and value propositions," International Journal of Information Management, vol. 43, pp. 224–247, 2018.
[14] P. M. Ferreira and M. A. Almeida, "Benefits and limitations of performance management systems in the public sector," Public Money & Management, vol. 35, no. 3, pp. 211–216, 2015.
[15] M. Ali and S. Wajidi, "Motivational Strategies and Employee Retention in IT Sector," International Journal of Management, vol. 12, no. 3, pp. 41–47, 2021.
[16] M. Ali and S. Wajidi, "Motivational Strategies and Employee Retention in IT Sector," International Journal of Management, vol. 12, no. 3, pp. 41–47, 2021.
[17] J. Kundu and B. Gahlawat, "Effects of organizational culture on employee retention: Empirical evidence from the Indian IT industry," Global Journal of Management and Business Research, vol. 16, no. 4, pp. 33–40, 2016.
[18] S. Tursunbayeva, M. Pagliari, and C. Di Lauro, "People analytics – A scoping review of conceptual boundaries and value propositions," International Journal of Information Management, vol. 43, pp. 224–247, 2018.
[19] P. M. Ferreira and M. A. Almeida, "Benefits and limitations of performance management systems in the public sector," Public Money & Management, vol. 35, no. 3, pp. 211–216, 2015.

Exploring the dimensions of Extended Reality

Ganesh Kumar M[1], Agam Das Goswami[2*]
[1]Assistant Professor, Department of E.C.E, QIS College of Engineering and Technology, Ongole, Andhra Pradesh, India.
[2]Associate Professor, School of Electronics Engineering, VIT-AP University, Amaravati, A.P, India.
mgani4111@gmail.com, agam.goswami@vitap.c.in

Abstract

Extended Reality (XR) is a revolutionary merger of the physical and virtual worlds, including Virtual Reality (VR), Augmented Reality (AR), and Mixed Reality (MR). This study explores the multifaceted dimensions of XR, which are rapidly redefining how we interact with digital environments. The study delves into the technological foundations of XR, examining the interplay of hardware, software, and human-computer interaction. It also addresses the potential of XR to revolutionize various sectors, including education, healthcare, entertainment, and remote collaboration, by offering immersive experiences that transcend traditional media boundaries. A key focus of this exploration is the analysis of XR's impact on user perception and cognition. By altering the way individuals perceive space and time, XR has the potential to enhance learning, improve therapeutic outcomes, and create new forms of entertainment. The abstract also considers the ethical and societal implications of XR, particularly in terms of privacy, accessibility, and the digital divide. As XR technologies continue to evolve, their ability to seamlessly blend physical and virtual realities will likely lead to unprecedented changes in how we live, work, and connect with the world. This exploration underscores the importance of interdisciplinary research in advancing XR, combining insights from computer science, psychology, design, and ethics. The study intends to contribute to a better understanding of XR's potential and limitations, laying the groundwork for future breakthroughs that will influence the next generation of digital experiences.

Keywords: Extended Reality, Virtual Reality, Augmented Reality, Mixed Reality, Environmental Sustainability.

1. Introduction

XR is an umbrella word for a variety of technologies that combine the physical and digital worlds. This spectrum encompasses VR, AR, and MR, all of which seek to improve our vision and engagement with the world around us. As XR technologies advance, they are becoming integral to various industries, including gaming, education, healthcare, and manufacturing, redefining how we experience and interact with reality [19].

In an era where the environmental consequences of human activity are under intense scrutiny, XR technologies offer both opportunities and challenges in the quest for sustainability [14]. On one hand, XR can significantly reduce the need for physical resources by enabling virtual meetings, training sessions, and simulations, which can cut down on travel, reduce carbon footprints, and lessen the reliance on material goods [16]. For example, businesses can use VR for remote collaboration, potentially minimizing the environmental impact associated with commuting and business travel.

On the other hand, the widespread adoption of XR technologies also brings about concerns related to energy consumption, electronic waste, and the carbon footprint of producing and maintaining

the necessary hardware. The energy demands of data centers powering XR experiences, the short life cycles of XR devices, and the need for high-performance computing power raise important questions about the long-term sustainability of these technologies [18].
This introduction explores the dual role of XR in environmental sustainability, examining how these technologies can contribute to reducing environmental impacts while also highlighting the potential challenges they pose. By understanding both sides, we can better leverage XR technologies to create a more sustainable future [1]. Fig. 1 shows the basic components of XR.

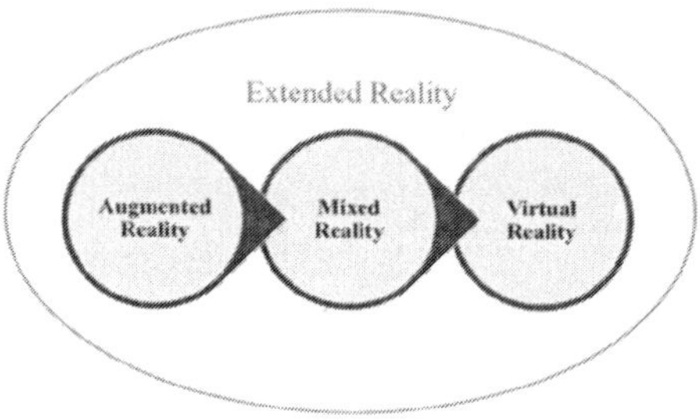

Fig. 1: Components of XR

1.1 The evolution of XR

The Origins of XR

The idea of losing oneself in a virtual world date back many years, to the 1960s, when Morton Heilig created the Sensorama, a mechanical apparatus that mimicked a multisensory environment. This early attempt at creating an immersive experience laid the groundwork for what would become VR. The development of XR has been driven by advances in computing power, display technologies, and motion tracking, leading to the sophisticated systems we have today [11].

Key Milestones

- **1968:** Ivan Sutherland develops the first head-mounted display (HMD), often regarded as the first VR device.
- **1992:** Tom Caudell coins the term "Augmented Reality," describing the overlay of digital information onto the physical world [9].
- **2010:** Palmer Luckey creates the Oculus Rift, a significant milestone in consumer VR.
- **2016:** Pokémon Go brings AR to the mainstream, demonstrating the potential of mobile AR experiences [2].
- **2020s:** The rise of 5G and cloud computing further propels the development of XR, enabling more complex and seamless experiences.

2. Literature Survey

XR technologies, which encompass VR, AR, and MR, have various implications for environmental sustainability. Here are some references that explore this intersection:

1. Stevens, J. et al (2020) discusses how VR can be used for environmental education and awareness.

2. Bonetti, F., Warnaby, G., & Quinn, L. et al (2018) examines the potential of AR and VR in reducing physical store footprints and thereby contributing to sustainability.
3. Fuchs, P., Moreau, G., & Guitton, P. et al (2011) provides foundational knowledge of VR technologies and includes discussions on potential environmental impacts.
4. Thompson, B., & Ribeiro, R. (2020) focuses on the life cycle analysis of XR technologies and their environmental footprint.
5. Moro, C., Štromberga, Z., Raikos, A., & Stirling, A. (2017) discusses the potential for reducing resource use in medical education through XR.
6. Duan, Y., Edwards, J. S., & Dwivedi, Y. K. (2019) explores the role of AI in optimizing XR for energy efficiency and reduced environmental impact.
7. Wang, P., Wu, P., Wang, J., Chi, H. L., & Wang, X. (2018) examines the use of VR in reducing waste and enhancing sustainability in construction.
8. Häfner, P., Häfner, V., &Ovtcharova, J. (2013) discusses the environmental benefits of using VR in education to minimize the need for physical materials.
9. Stahl, B. C., Timmermans, J., & Flick, C. (2017) explores ethical implications of XR technologies, including environmental sustainability.
10. Ishii, K., & Watanabe, T. (2019) reviews how VR can be used to promote conservation and sustainable practices.
11. Zhou, F., Duh, H. B. L., & Billinghurst, M. (2008) discusses advancements in AR and their implications for sustainability.
12. Cruz-Neira, C., Sandin, D. J., & DeFanti, T. A. (1993) introduces CAVE, an immersive VR environment, and discusses its potential to reduce environmental impact in research and training.
13. McCann, B. T., & Brynjolfsson, E. (2017) looks at the use of machine learning to optimize XR experiences for sustainability in retail.
14. Baumeister, R. F., & Leary, M. R. (1995) explores how VR can satisfy human social needs while reducing the environmental costs of physical interactions.
15. Pujol, L., & Champion, E. (2012) examines the role of VR in preserving cultural heritage sites, potentially reducing the environmental impact of tourism [15].
16. Minocha, S., & Reeves, A. J. (2010) discusses how virtual worlds can be designed to promote environmental sustainability.
17. Calderon, E., & Ruiz, M. (2015) focuses on the educational potential of VR in fostering environmental sustainability.
18. Lee, K. M., & Noh, S. D. (2016) explores how AR can be used in manufacturing to reduce waste and improve energy efficiency.
19. Fowler, C. (2015) discusses the use of VR in educational settings to minimize the environmental impact of traditional learning methods.
20. Sanders, E. B. N., &Stappers, P. J. (2008) looks at the role of co-creation in XR design and its implications for sustainable development.

3. The Spectrum of XR

3.1 Virtual Reality

VR uses head-mounted displays (HMDs) and motion controllers to immerse users in a fully digital world [3][6]. VR experiences can range from fully interactive environments in video games to virtual tours of real-world locations [17]. The technology is widely used in gaming, training simulations, and therapy, offering users an escape from the physical world into a completely virtual one.

- **Applications:** Gaming, training simulations, therapy, education [7].
- **Challenges:** Motion sickness, the requirement for high-end hardware, and limited real-world interaction.

3.2 Augmented Reality

Augmented Reality (AR) enhances the user's environment without totally replacing it by superimposing digital content over the real world. AR is often delivered through smartphones, tablets, or specialized glasses like the Microsoft HoloLens [4]. Applications of AR are vast, ranging from entertainment and retail to navigation and education [8].

- **Applications:** Navigation, education, retail, industrial maintenance.
- **Challenges:** Limited field of view, accuracy of digital overlays, and the need for powerful mobile devices.

3.3 Mixed Reality

MR creates environments where digital and physical objects coexist and interact in real time by fusing the physical and digital worlds. With tools like the HoloLens 2 allowing users to interact digital things as if they were real, mixed reality (MR) is frequently viewed as a more immersive version of augmented reality (AR).

- **Applications:** Design and prototyping, collaborative workspaces, advanced training simulations [12].
- **Challenges:** High cost of MR devices, limited content, and technological complexity.

4. Technological components of XR

4.1 Hardware

The hardware that powers XR experiences includes HMDs, motion controllers, haptic feedback devices, and spatial tracking systems. Each piece of hardware plays a critical role in creating a seamless and immersive experience.

- **Head-Mounted Displays (HMDs):** Devices like the Oculus Rift, HTC Vive, and PlayStation VR that cover the user's eyes and ears to immerse them in a virtual environment.
- **Motion Controllers:** Devices that let users interact with the virtual environment, such as the Oculus Touch controllers.
- **Haptic Feedback:** Technology that simulates touch, enhancing the realism of XR experiences.
- **Spatial Tracking:** Real-time tracking systems for users to make sure the digital material reacts appropriately to their movements.

4.2 Software

The software component of XR includes the platforms and engines that power the creation and delivery of XR experiences. This includes game engines like Unity and Unreal Engine, which are used to develop VR and AR experiences, as well as specialized AR software like ARKit (Apple) and ARCore (Google).

- **Game Engines:** Unity, Unreal Engine.
- **AR Platforms:** ARKit, ARCore, Vuforia.
- **MR Software:** Microsoft MR Toolkit, Magic Leap SDK.

5. Applications of XR

5.1 Gaming and Entertainment

The gaming industry has been a major driver of XR adoption, with VR games offering immersive experiences that were previously unimaginable. AR games like Pokémon Go have demonstrated the potential for mobile-based experiences that blend the real and digital worlds.

- **VR Gaming:** Fully immersive experiences in digital worlds.
- **AR Gaming:** Games that interact with the real world.
- **MR Entertainment:** Interactive experiences in theme parks and museums.

5.2 Education and Training

XR is transforming education by providing immersive learning experiences that engage students in new ways. Virtual classrooms, AR textbooks, and MR training simulations are just a few examples of how XR is being used to enhance education.

- **Virtual Classrooms:** Immersive environments for distance learning.
- **AR Textbooks:** Interactive learning materials that bring subjects to life.
- **Training Simulations:** Safe and realistic environments for training in fields like medicine and aviation.

5.3 Healthcare

In healthcare, XR is being used for everything from surgical simulations to patient rehabilitation. VR is helping to train the next generation of surgeons, while AR is being used to guide procedures in real-time.

- **Surgical Simulations:** VR environments for practicing complex procedures.
- **Rehabilitation:** XR-based therapies for physical and mental health.
- **Medical Imaging:** AR overlays for enhanced visualization of patient data [5].

5.4 Industrial Applications

Industries such as manufacturing, automotive, and construction are leveraging XR for design, prototyping, and maintenance. MR allows engineers to collaborate on complex designs, while AR provides technicians with real-time information during repairs [20].

- **Design and Prototyping:**Collaborative design spaces and virtual prototypes.
- **Maintenance and Repair:** AR-guided instructions for complex tasks.
- **Safety Training:** Immersive simulations for hazardous environments.

6. Obstacles and prospects for the future

6.1 Technical Challenges

Despite its potential, XR faces several technical challenges. These include the need for more powerful hardware, better spatial tracking, and improved user interfaces. Additionally, issues like motion sickness and limited field of view continue to hinder widespread adoption.

6.2 Ethical and Social Implications

XR presents significant moral and societal issues as it spreads. It is necessary to address worries about data security, privacy, and addiction potential. Moreover, the impact of XR on social interactions and mental health must be carefully considered.

6.3 The Future of XR

As technology develops, there are many exciting prospects for XR in the future. These immersive encounters will become more commonplace as XR devices become more widely available and reasonably priced. Artificial intelligence (AI) and machine learning (ML) developments will improve XR even further, personalizing and streamlining interactions. But the growing use of XR also brings up issues like data privacy, the digital divide, and the risk of relying too much on virtual surroundings. In order to guarantee that XR technologies are created and used ethically, it will be imperative to address these concerns.

7. Impact of extended reality technologies on environmental sustainability

XR technologies, which include VR, AR, and MR, are rapidly evolving and have significant implications for environmental sustainability [10][13][22]. Their impact can be both positive and negative, depending on how they are developed, deployed, and integrated into society.

7.1 Positive Impacts on Environmental Sustainability

Reduction in Carbon Footprint:

- **Remote Work and Virtual Meetings**: XR enables immersive remote work environments, reducing the need for physical travel. This can significantly cut down carbon emissions associated with commuting and business travel.
- **Virtual Events**: XR technologies can host large-scale events like conferences, exhibitions, and concerts virtually, reducing the environmental impact of physical events, including travel, accommodation, and waste generation [21].

Enhanced Environmental Awareness and Education:

- **Immersive Environmental Education**: XR can create highly engaging simulations that allow users to experience the impact of environmental degradation or the benefits of sustainable practices firsthand. This can increase awareness and drive behavioral change towards more sustainable lifestyles.
- **Virtual Conservation Efforts**: XR can simulate natural habitats and ecosystems, providing a platform for education and virtual tourism. This reduces the need for physical interaction with sensitive environments, aiding in their preservation.

Design and Testing:

- **Sustainable Product Design**: XR can be used in product design and testing, allowing companies to prototype and iterate without the need for physical materials. This reduces waste and the environmental impact of traditional manufacturing processes.
- **Urban Planning**: XR technologies can aid in the visualization of sustainable urban designs, enabling planners to optimize city layouts for energy efficiency, green spaces, and reduced pollution.

Behavioral Change:

- **Sustainable Consumer Choices**: XR can help consumers make more sustainable choices by providing information on product lifecycle impacts or simulating the environmental benefits of certain actions, such as recycling or using renewable energy.

7.2 Negative Impacts on Environmental Sustainability

Energy Consumption:

- **High Energy Demand**: VR and other XR technologies demand a lot of processing power, which results in high energy consumption. Data centres powering XR applications also contribute to energy use, potentially offsetting some of the environmental benefits.
- **Hardware Production**: The production of XR hardware, such as VR headsets, requires resources and energy. The frequent updates and short lifecycle of technology products can lead to increased electronic waste (e-waste).

Electronic Waste:

- **Short Lifespan of Devices**: XR devices, like many electronic products, have relatively short lifespans and become obsolete quickly, contributing to e-waste. Proper recycling and disposal of these devices are essential to minimize environmental impact.
- **Resource Extraction**: Rare earth metals and other resources must be extracted in order to produce XR hardware, which can have a negative influence on the environment due to pollution, habitat destruction, and increased carbon emissions.

Data Center Emissions:

- **Cloud and Streaming Services**: XR applications often rely on cloud computing and streaming services, which require data centers. These centers consume large amounts of electricity, often from non-renewable sources, contributing to greenhouse gas emissions.

7.3 Strategies for Enhancing the Positive Impact of XR on Sustainability

Energy Efficiency:

- **Develop Energy-Efficient Hardware**: Innovating energy-efficient XR devices and optimizing software to reduce computational demands can help lower the overall energy consumption of XR technologies.
- **Use of Renewable Energy**: Powering data centers and production facilities with renewable energy can significantly reduce the carbon footprint associated with XR technologies.

Sustainable Product Lifecycle:

- **Design for Longevity and Repairability**: XR devices should be designed with durability in mind, allowing for easy repairs and upgrades to extend their lifespan and reduce e-waste.
- **Recycling Programs**: Implementing robust recycling programs for XR devices can help mitigate the impact of electronic waste.

Responsible Production:

- **Sustainable Material Sourcing**: Sourcing materials responsibly and minimizing the environmental impact of extraction processes can help reduce the overall ecological footprint of XR technologies.

8. Conclusion

XR is a fundamental change in the way we engage with the world, not merely a fad in technology. As XR continues to evolve, it will undoubtedly unlock new possibilities across industries, changing the way we experience reality itself. By understanding the current landscape of XR, we can better prepare for the opportunities and challenges that lie ahead. XR technologies have the potential to support environmental sustainability through various applications, from reducing carbon footprints to enhancing education and promoting sustainable behaviors. However, challenges such as energy consumption, e-waste, and resource extraction must be addressed to fully realize their benefits. With careful consideration and sustainable practices, XR can contribute positively to global sustainability efforts.

References

1. Stevens, J. (2020). "Virtual Reality and the Environment: A New Way to Engage with Sustainability." Journal of Environmental Management, 258, 110022.
2. Bonetti, F., Warnaby, G., & Quinn, L. (2018). "Augmented Reality and Virtual Reality in Physical and Online Retailing: A Review, Synthesis, and Research Agenda." Journal of Business Research, 100, 581-589.
3. Fuchs, P., Moreau, G., & Guitton, P. (2011). "Virtual Reality: Concepts and Technologies." CRC Press.
4. Thompson, B., & Ribeiro, R. (2020). "The Environmental Impacts of Virtual and Augmented Reality." Environmental Research Letters, 15(11), 113004.
5. Moro, C., Štromberga, Z., Raikos, A., & Stirling, A. (2017). "The Effectiveness of Virtual and Augmented Reality in Health Sciences and Medical Anatomy." Anatomical Sciences Education, 10(6), 549-559.
6. Duan, Y., Edwards, J. S., & Dwivedi, Y. K. (2019). "Artificial Intelligence for Decision Making in the Era of Big Data – Evolution, Challenges, and Research Agenda." International Journal of Information Management, 48, 63-71.
7. Wang, P., Wu, P., Wang, J., Chi, H. L., & Wang, X. (2018). "A Critical Review of the Use of Virtual Reality in Construction Engineering Education and Training." International Journal of Environmental Research and Public Health, 15(6), 1204.
8. Häfner, P., Häfner, V., &Ovtcharova, J. (2013). "Teaching Methodology for Virtual Reality Practical Course in Engineering Education." Procedia Computer Science, 25, 251-260.
9. Stahl, B. C., Timmermans, J., & Flick, C. (2017). "Ethics of Emerging Information and Communication Technologies: On the Implementation of Responsible Research and Innovation." Science and Public Policy, 44(3), 369-381.
10. Ishii, K., & Watanabe, T. (2019). "Impact of Virtual Reality on Conservation and Sustainability: A Review." Sustainability, 11(12), 3314.
11. Zhou, F., Duh, H. B. L., & Billinghurst, M. (2008). "Trends in Augmented Reality Tracking, Interaction, and Display: A Review of Ten Years of ISMAR." Proceedings of the 7th IEEE/ACM International Symposium on Mixed and Augmented Reality (ISMAR), 193-202.
12. Cruz-Neira, C., Sandin, D. J., & DeFanti, T. A. (1993). "Surround-Screen Projection-Based Virtual Reality: The Design and Implementation of the CAVE." Proceedings of the 20th Annual Conference on Computer Graphics and Interactive Techniques, 135-142.
13. McCann, B. T., & Brynjolfsson, E. (2017). "Machine Learning in Retail: Powering Customer Satisfaction in the Emerging AR and VR Age." MIT Sloan Management Review, 58(4), 57-65.
14. Baumeister, R. F., & Leary, M. R. (1995). "The Need to Belong: Desire for Interpersonal Attachments as a Fundamental Human Motivation." Psychological Bulletin, 117(3), 497-529.
15. Pujol, L., & Champion, E. (2012). "Evaluating Presence in Cultural Heritage Projects." International Journal of Heritage in the Digital Era, 1(2), 288-305.
16. Minocha, S., & Reeves, A. J. (2010). "Designing for Inclusion: The Effect of Virtual Worlds on Environmental Perception." International Journal of Architectural Computing, 8(1), 1-16.
17. Calderon, E., & Ruiz, M. (2015). "The Role of Virtual Reality in Education: The Case of Environmental Sustainability." Procedia Environmental Sciences, 30, 389-395.

18. Lee, K. M., & Noh, S. D. (2016). "Applying Augmented Reality to Manufacturing and Service Operations for Environmental Sustainability." Journal of Cleaner Production, 113, 366-376.
19. Fowler, C. (2015). "Virtual Reality and Learning: Trends and Issues." Emerging Trends in ICT for Education and Training, 8, 137-146.
20. Sanders, E. B. N., &Stappers, P. J. (2008). "Co-Creation and the New Landscapes of Design." Co-Design, 4(1), 5-18.
21. J. Moodley et al., "Beyond Reality: An Application of Extended Reality and Blockchain in the Metaverse," 2023 IEEE International Conference on Omni-layer Intelligent Systems (COINS), Berlin, Germany, 2023, pp. 1-4, doi: 10.1109/COINS57856.2023.10189285.
22. S. Zhang and W. Li, "Applying eXtended Reality (XR) Technology in Commerce, Management, and Business Applications: A Survey," 2024 4th International Conference on Computer, Control and Robotics (ICCCR), Shnaghai, China, 2024, pp. 108-113, doi: 10.1109/ICCCR61138.2024.10585599.
23. T. Moser, J. Wolfartsberger, S. R. Sorko and B. Abu Naim, "Extended Reality Based Education and Training for Human-Centric Industry 5.0 Skill Enhancement," NOMS 2024-2024 IEEE Network Operations and Management Symposium, Seoul, Korea, Republic of, 2024, pp. 1-4, doi: 10.1109/NOMS59830.2024.10575896.

- **Circular Economy Models**: Encouraging a circular economy, where XR devices [23] are reused, refurbished, or recycled, can help reduce the demand for new resources and decrease waste.

TROJAN VIRUS

Mr Jagadeeswara Rao Palisetti*, Sr. Assistant Professor, LBRCE, Mylavaram,521230, pjagadeeswararao@gmail.ac.in, pjr@lbrce.ac.in
Mrs Shaik Razeena Begum, Sr. Assistant Professor, LBRCE, Mylavaram,521230, razeenabegum@gmail.com
Dr Shaik Jameer, Associate Professor, LBRCE, Mylavaram,521230, jameer.sk4u@gmail.com
M.Sreeram, IIIrd Year Student, LBRCE, Mylavaram,521230.
S.Teja Sai, IIIrd Year Student, LBRCE, Mylavaram,521230.

Abstract
In order to trick users into installing or running malicious software on their systems, a Trojan virus, also known as a Trojan horse, poses as trustworthy or harmless software. Trojans rely on social engineering techniques or software flaws to obtain access, unlike viruses and worms, which replicate themselves. Trojans use their covert payload, which may involve ransomware deployment, data theft, backdoor development, or system compromise, once they have gained access to a system.

The architecture of a Trojan virus often contains a user-friendly interface or legitimate functions to prevent suspicion, combined with covert destructive code. This dual nature helps it to elude discovery during early contacts. Modern Trojans have evolved to include extensive evasion strategies including polymorphism, encryption, and rootkit components, making them more difficult to identify and remove. Trojans can wreak extensive damage to individuals, businesses, and even nations. They frequently act as a backdoor for broader cyberattacks, such as espionage, financial fraud, and infrastructure damage. Banking Trojans, which are meant to steal financial information, and Remote Access Trojans (RATs), which allow attackers to take control of infected systems, are two notable instances.

This abstract highlight contemporary detection and mitigation techniques while examining the lifecycle of Trojan viruses, from activation and propagation to their ultimate consequence. Although technologies like machine learning, heuristic detection, and behavioural analysis have demonstrated potential in thwarting these threats, the swift development of Trojan horses demands ongoing improvements in cybersecurity defences. Building strong defences and guaranteeing digital safety in a world growing more interconnected requires an understanding of the fundamental workings of Trojan infections and their place in the larger cyber threat ecosystem.

Introduction

The Trojan virus, also known as a Trojan horse, is a dishonest kind of malicious software (malware) that poses as trustworthy or helpful software to fool users into running it. This kind of malware, which takes its name from the Trojan Horse myth in ancient Greece, works on the principle of concealment, seeming harmless on the outside but carrying malicious intent. Unlike self-replicating malware such as worms and viruses, Trojans rely on user action or exploitation of weaknesses to infiltrate systems.

Trojans have become one of the most ubiquitous and versatile hazards in the digital realm. They are widely used as a vector for several malicious operations, including unauthorized access, data theft, ransomware deployment, and the development of backdoors into infected systems. They are especially dangerous because of their ability to pass for genuine apps, which allows attackers to get beyond conventional security measures and secretly carry out their payloads.

Because of their constantly changing nature and the addition of sophisticated tactics like encryption, polymorphism, and stealth mechanisms, Trojan horses present a significant challenge to cybersecurity experts. Trojans can avoid detection, remain in compromised systems, and adjust to defences thanks to these features. Understanding the workings and ramifications of Trojan infections is essential for people, businesses, and governments alike as cyber attacks continue to increase in complexity and scope. The basic traits of Trojan viruses, their modes of operation, and their place in the larger cybersecurity environment are all covered in this introduction. This section lays the groundwork for a thorough examination of their lifetime, detection techniques, and mitigation tactics by looking at their impact and the difficulties they provide.

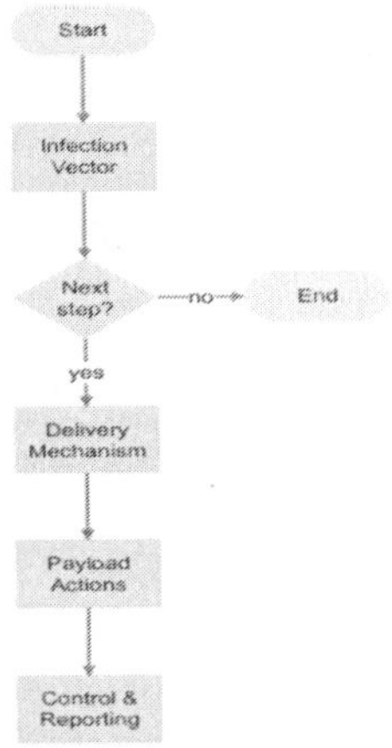

Review and Challenges in Trojan Viruses

Trojan viruses have evolved into a major cybersecurity danger, using sophisticated tactics to enter computers and carry out harmful actions. This review investigates their growth, important characteristics, and obstacles in combating them.

Review of Trojan Viruses

1. Evolution and Functionality Trojans have evolved from simple malicious programs into sophisticated dangers capable of eluding detection. Early versions were unsophisticated, frequently posing as benign files. Modern variations use polymorphic code, encryption, and stealth tactics to circumvent security systems.

2. Common Types of Trojans

- **Banking Trojans:** Target financial information by taking advantage of holes in online banking systems.
- **Remote Access Trojans (RATs)**: Give hackers command over compromised systems to facilitate data theft and surveillance.
- **Ransomware Trojans**: Demand payment to decode the victims' data after it has been encrypted.
- **Downloader Trojans**: Act as entry points for other malicious software.

3. Propagation Methods Trojan horses propagate via fraudulent websites, phishing emails, infected software, and pirated material. The major technique for tricking consumers into downloading these dangers is still social engineering.

Challenges in Addressing Trojan Viruses

1. Advanced Evasion Techniques To conceal their existence, modern Trojan horses use rootkit components, encryption, and obfuscation. Dynamically changing its code, polymorphic Trojans make detection more difficult.

2. Increasing Sophistication Attackers have developed Trojans that adjust to defensive tactics by combining artificial intelligence and machine learning, which reduces the effectiveness of conventional antivirus software.

3. Wide Attack Surface The number of possible Trojan targets has increased due to the growth of cloud computing, remote work settings, and Internet of Things (IoT) devices. These platforms are insecure because they frequently lack strong security measures.

4. Human Error Even the most sophisticated technologies are unable to eliminate the risk provided by inexperienced users, and social engineering takes advantage of human nature.

5. Resource-Intensive Countermeasures It takes a lot of resources to develop and implement advanced cybersecurity solutions like behavioral analysis, heuristic-based detection, and AI-driven monitoring.

Challenges in Trojan Viruses (Table)

Challenge	Description	Implications	Potential Mitigations
Evasion Techniques	Use of encryption, polymorphism, and rootkits to evade detection.	Reduces effectiveness of traditional antivirus and signature-based detection.	Behavioral analysis, heuristic detection, and advanced machine learning models.
Social Engineering	Relies on deceiving users into executing the Trojan.	Makes user awareness and training critical to prevention.	Enhanced user education and awareness campaigns about phishing and malicious downloads.
Rapid Evolution	Continuous development of new variants and strains.	Stays ahead of signature updates in security software.	Real-time threat intelligence and proactive security updates.
Targeted Attacks	Customization for specific industries, organizations, or individuals.	Increases impact and reduces likelihood of early detection.	Threat hunting and industry-specific cybersecurity solutions.
Multi-Stage Attacks	Use of Trojans as an initial vector for more extensive attacks, such as ransomware or Advanced Persistent Threats (APTs).	Escalates potential damage and makes recovery more complex.	Network segmentation, endpoint detection and response (EDR), and layered security architectures.

Challenge	Description	Implications	Potential Mitigations
Insufficient Detection Mechanisms	Difficulty in identifying Trojans due to their resemblance to legitimate software.	Allows Trojans to operate undetected for prolonged periods.	Zero-trust security models, enhanced sandboxing, and automated behavioral analysis tools.

Advantages and Limitations in Trojan Viruses

Advantages (from the perspective of attackers)

Cybercriminals favor Trojan infections because of their adaptability and stealth. Some of their main "advantages" (as seen by attackers) are listed below:

1. **Stealth and Concealment:** Trojan viruses are preferred by cybercriminals due to their versatility and secrecy. The following are some of their primary "advantages" as seen by attackers:
2. **Customizability:**
   Trojans can be customized by attackers for certain uses, such espionage, system disruption, or data theft.
3. **Diverse Attack Vectors:** Trojan horses can propagate via several channels, including as fraudulent websites, software downloads, and email attachments.
4. **Multi-Stage Attacks:** Trojan horses may serve as gateways for more sophisticated malware, including botnets or ransomware.
5. **Persistence:**
   Certain Trojans use techniques like rootkits or self-repair capabilities to keep control of a machine even after detection attempts.
6. **Exploitation of Human Vulnerabilities:** Trojans can increase the efficacy of security mechanisms by manipulating people to circumvent them through social engineering.

Limitations (from the perspective of attackers)

Despite their benefits, Trojan horses have some drawbacks that shorten their lifespan or overall efficacy:

1. **Dependence on User Interaction:** Trojans frequently require the user to run them, for example, by opening a file or an attachment.
2. **Detection and Mitigation Advances:** Trojans are becoming more and more detectable with the use of behavioral analysis and modern antivirus software, particularly when paired with machine learning.
3. **Lack of Self-Replication:** Trojan horses, in contrast to viruses or worms, require intentional replication techniques and are unable to spread on their own.
4. **Network Restrictions:** Trojans' effectiveness and ability to proliferate within a targeted context are restricted by network segmentation and zero-trust designs.
5. **Exposure Risk:** Once a Trojan's signature has been found, it can be included in threat databases, which will make future attacks less successful.
6. **Dependency on Vulnerabilities:** Users that patch and upgrade their operating systems and applications on a regular basis can reduce the effectiveness of Trojan horses.

Applications of Trojan Viruses

Trojan viruses are typically utilized by attackers as malicious tools, although depending on the perpetrator's goal, they can be used for a number of purposes. The following list of typical Trojan virus uses is arranged according to their function:

---

1. Data Theft

- **Objective:** stealing private information, including financial information, login passwords, intellectual property, or personal information.
- **Examples:** In order to compromise online banking credentials, banking Trojans (such as Zeus and Dridex) are made to record keystrokes, screenshots, and other input.

---

2. Remote Access and Control

- **Objective:** Giving hackers the ability to take over compromised systems and obtain illegal access.
- **Examples:** Attackers can utilize Remote Access Trojans (RATs) to change files, install more malware, or even spy on users via a webcam or microphone.

---

3. System Damage or Disruption

- **Objective:** Destroying, encrypting, or corrupting data in order to interfere with operations or make systems unusable.
- **Examples:** Trojan horses that encrypt data and demand money for decryption keys are employed in ransomware attacks like WannaCry.

---

4. Botnet Creation

- **Objective:** Creating a network of compromised devices (botnets) by breaking into several systems to launch coordinated attacks.
- **Examples:** Botnets are frequently used for sending massive amounts of spam or for Distributed Denial of Service (DDoS) attacks.

---

5. Cyber Espionage

- **Objective:** spying on specific people, groups, or countries to obtain private information.
- **Examples:** Trojan horses are used by Advanced Persistent Threats (APTs) to set up long-term monitoring and data exfiltration systems.

---

6. Propagation of Other Malware

- **Objective:** serving as a conduit for more complex or specialized malware.
- **Examples:** Additional malware, like ransomware, spyware, or adware, is installed on the compromised system via downloader Trojans.

---

7. Monetary Gain

- **Objective:** Making money by coercion, fraud, or other financial schemes.
- **Examples:** Investing in banking While cryptocurrency mining Trojans surreptitiously use the victim's resources to mine digital coins, online banking systems are the target of Trojan horses.

---

8. Sabotage

- **Objective:** intentionally upsetting or harming systems, frequently for ideological or political reasons.
- **Examples:** Stuxnet, although not a classic Trojan, used Trojan-like features to sabotage industrial control systems.

Case Study: Zeus Trojan Virus

Overview

One of the most well-known and extensively disseminated malware strains is the Zeus Trojan, sometimes referred to as Zbot, which is mostly used to steal personal data and banking passwords. Since its first discovery in 2007, it has undergone multiple variations and grown to pose a serious threat to people and organizations all across the world.

Background

Zeus was created as a toolset for crimeware, enabling hackers to craft personalized malware variants. It frequently spreads via phishing emails, malware attachments, and compromised websites and targets Windows operating systems. In order to obtain instructions and exfiltrate stolen data, Zeus usually installs itself on victims' computers and establishes a connection with a command and control (C&C) server.

Key Features

- **Keylogging:**
  Zeus records sensitive data, including credit card numbers, usernames, and passwords, by capturing keystrokes.
- **Form Grabbing:** It is especially useful against online banking operations because it can intercept web forms and record user-inputted data.
- **Web Injection:** Zeus can change the content of websites that infected users visit, forcing them to provide more information that the Trojan can exploit to obtain it.
- **Modular Architecture:** The Trojan's architecture permits the installation of many plugins, enabling functions like remote access and additional system exploitation.
- **Persistence:** Zeus uses rootkits to conceal its processes and registry modifications to keep itself active on compromised computers.

Impact

Zeus has had a huge impact, causing both individuals and businesses to suffer large financial losses. Millions of dollars' worth of stolen money was made possible by its capacity to steal banking passwords. For instance, it was revealed in 2010 that the Zeus Trojan had embezzled approximately $70 million from American institutions.

Because the Zeus Trojan was so ubiquitous, law enforcement organizations responded globally, launching a concerted effort called Operation Trident to take down the infrastructure that the malware was using. Several people connected to the distribution of Zeus were arrested as a result of this operation.

Mitigation and Response

Organizations and individuals have adopted a number of mitigation techniques to counter the threat posed by Zeus, such as:

1. **Enhanced Security Measures:** To prevent unwanted transactions, banks and other financial institutions have enhanced their fraud detection systems and implemented multi-factor authentication.
2. **User Education:** To prevent infection, it is now essential to raise knowledge about phishing schemes and secure browsing techniques.
3. **Regular Software Updates:** Updating OS systems and antivirus software reduces vulnerabilities that Zeus and related viruses can exploit.
4. **Threat Intelligence Sharing:** Tracking and interfering with Zeus operations has required cooperation between law enforcement and groups to exchange threat intelligence.

Conclusion

In the field of cybersecurity, the Zeus Trojan is an engaging case study that emphasizes the intricacies of contemporary malware and the ongoing arms race between attackers and defenses. Its effects highlight how crucial it is to have strong security procedures, educate users, and work together to counteract changing threats in the digital world. The lessons from the Zeus case are still applicable for creating strong defenses against upcoming cyberthreats as malware keeps evolving.

Conclusion on Trojan Viruses

Trojan viruses are a serious and constantly changing concern in the field of cybersecurity because they utilize deceit to get inside systems and carry out harmful tasks. They are difficult to detect and prevent because of their architecture, which frequently hides malicious payloads inside programs that appear to be legal. Trojans continue to have a widespread influence on people, businesses, and even governmental agencies around the world as fraudsters develop and adapt.

Trojan infections can have serious repercussions, including compromised sensitive data, financial losses, and data breaches. The threat is increased by their capacity to serve as carriers of additional malware, leading to intricate and multidimensional intrusions. The case studies of well-known Trojans, like Zeus, emphasize the necessity of proactive protection measures and constant attention to detail.

Adopting a thorough cybersecurity approach that include user education, frequent software upgrades, the use of cutting-edge detection tools, and a proactive incident response plan is crucial to reducing the hazards posed by Trojan viruses. In order to share threat intelligence and create efficient countermeasures, cooperation between stakeholders—including law enforcement and private sector organizations—is essential.

Trojan viruses will probably continue to pose a hazard as technology advances and the digital world grows more interconnected. Thus, it is essential to comprehend their workings, ramifications, and defense mechanisms in order to protect digital assets belonging to individuals and organizations from this advanced type of malware.

Future Scope of Trojan Viruses

The field of cybersecurity is always changing, and the future reach of Trojan viruses is a reflection of both technological breakthroughs and the flexible tactics used by cybercriminals. It is anticipated that Trojan viruses will become more sophisticated and complex as people and organizations strengthen their defenses. The following are some possible advancements in Trojan virus research in the future:

1. **Increased Use of Artificial Intelligence and Machine Learning**
    - **Description:** Cybercriminals may use machine learning algorithms and artificial intelligence (AI) to create increasingly sophisticated Trojan horses that may modify their behavior in response to real-time security measure assessments.
    - **Implications:** Trojans that are more adept at avoiding detection, customizing attacks, and optimizing impact may result from this.

2. **Targeted Attacks and Customization**
    - **Description:** It is probable that attackers will continue to tailor Trojans to take advantage of known flaws or vulnerabilities in certain industries or organizations, such as healthcare or finance.
    - **Implications:** To reduce the risk of targeted Trojan assaults, organizations will need to improve their threat intelligence capabilities and customize their defenses.

3. **Integration with IoT Devices**
    - **Description:** Trojans may target connected devices more frequently as the Internet of Things (IoT) grows, taking advantage of their flaws to access networks or private information.
    - **Implications:** This could lead to broader security implications as more devices become compromised, necessitating the need for stringent security measures for IoT environments.

4. **Evolution of Ransomware Techniques**
    - **Description:** Trojans will probably increasingly combine their methods with ransomware, encrypting data in addition to stealing it and then demanding a ransom.
    - **Implications:** Organizations will face challenging recovery scenarios as a result of this combined threat, underscoring the necessity of thorough backup and recovery plans.

5. **Stealthier Evasion Techniques**
    - **Description:** Future Trojans might use more sophisticated evasion strategies, like file less malware, rootkit functionality, and polymorphic code, which would make them harder to identify.
    - **Implications:** To combat these covert tactics, security solutions will need to change and use anomaly detection and behavioral analysis.

6. **Regulatory and Compliance Changes**
    - **Description:** Governments and regulatory agencies may impose more stringent cybersecurity laws and compliance standards as the threat landscape changes to safeguard sensitive information and vital infrastructure.
    - **Implications:** To reduce the risks of Trojan infections, organizations must maintain compliance and be informed about regulatory changes.

7. **Enhanced Collaboration and Information Sharing**
    - **Description:** To share threat intelligence and create group defense plans against Trojan threats, cybersecurity experts, law enforcement, and corporations will need to work together more.

- **Implications:** This will strengthen the overall cybersecurity posture and increase the capacity to react to new threats.

References:

1. **Symantec Threat Intelligence Reports**
   - Symantec frequently publishes reports on emerging threats, including detailed analyses of malware like Trojan viruses. Their annual "Internet Security Threat Report" offers insights into trends and statistics.
   - Symantec Threat Report
2. **McAfee Labs Threat Reports**
   - McAfee Labs provides comprehensive reports on malware trends, including information about Trojans and their impact on cybersecurity.
   - McAfee Labs Threat Center
3. **Kaspersky Security Bulletin**
   - Kaspersky's security bulletins provide analysis of Trojan viruses and other malware threats, including case studies and evolving techniques used by cybercriminals.
   - Kaspersky Security Bulletin
4. **Cisco Annual Cybersecurity Report**
   - Cisco's reports often cover the evolving nature of cyber threats, including Trojans, their architecture, and trends in malware distribution.
   - Cisco Cybersecurity Reports
5. **IBM X-Force Threat Intelligence Index**
   - IBM's X-Force Index provides insights into the current threat landscape, including analysis of various malware types, including Trojans.
   - IBM X-Force Threat Intelligence
6. **"Malware: A Beginner's Guide" by John R. Vacca**
   - This book covers various malware types, including Trojans, providing an understanding of their functionality and impact on cybersecurity.
   - ISBN: 978-0071799435
7. **"Cybersecurity Essentials" by Charles J. Brooks et al.**
   - This textbook includes chapters on malware, including Trojans, and offers insights into prevention and mitigation strategies.
   - ISBN: 978-0134851890
8. **Research Articles and Journals**
   - Many cybersecurity journals and conferences publish research on malware analysis, Trojan detection, and countermeasures. Look for journals like the Journal of Computer Virology and Hacking Techniques and proceedings from the ACM Conference on Computer and Communications Security.
9. **National Institute of Standards and Technology (NIST)**
   - NIST provides resources and guidelines on cybersecurity, including information on malware threats and protective measures.
   - NIST Cybersecurity Framework

10. **Government Cybersecurity Agencies**
   - Agencies such as the Cybersecurity and Infrastructure Security Agency (CISA) in the U.S. provide resources and alerts regarding malware threats, including Trojans.
   - CISA Alerts

MYCIN

Mr Sivanagaraju Vallabhuni*, Sr. Assistant Professor, LBRCE, Mylavaram, 521230, snraju164@gmail.com
Dr Shaik Jameer, Associate Professor, LBRCE, Mylavaram, 521230, jameer.sk4u@gmail.com
Dr Shaik Salma Asiya Begum, Associate Professor, LBRCE, Mylavaram, 521230, salma.ahu172@gmail.com
Bommareddy Raghav Reddy, IIIrd Year Student, LBRCE, Mylavaram, 521230.
Shaik Khaja Mahammed Hussain, IIIrd Year Student, LBRCE, Mylavaram, 521230.

ABSTRACT:
Originally created at Stanford University in the 1970s for the detection and treatment of bacterial infections, especially with an eye towards infectious disorders like meningitis and bacteraemia, MYCIN was an early expert system. MYCIN modelled the decision-making process of medical professionals using a rule-based methodology. It comprised an inference engine using forward and backward chaining to provide diagnosis and treatment recommendations and a knowledge base with over 500 rules drawn from clinical experience. Usually working professionals, the system asked pertinent questions, analysed the answers, and provided guidance on suitable antibiotic dosages and options. Although MYCIN was not extensively used in reality, it showed the possibilities of artificial intelligence in medicine and prepared the foundation for the creation of increasingly complex expert systems.

INTRODUCTION: -

Overview of MYCIN Expert System:

MYCIN was an early artificial intelligence (AI)-based expert system created in the 1970s at Stanford University. It was created to aid medical practitioners in identifying and treating infectious disorders, notably bacterial infections like meningitis and bacteremia. MYCIN became one of the most renowned instances of rule-based expert systems, which leverage a knowledge base of domain-specific expertise to replicate human reasoning.

Key Features of MYCIN:

1. **Rule-Based Reasoning**: MYCIN employed a collection of approximately 500 "if-then" rules, which reflected the expertise of medical specialists. These criteria were used to form conclusions based on patient data. For example, if a patient presented particular symptoms and test findings, MYCIN would utilise the applicable criteria to make a diagnosis and offer treatment.
2. **Knowledge Base:** The system's information was stored in the form of rules, which were drawn from medical specialists' expertise and experience. This knowledge base was regularly updated to increase the system's accuracy.
3. **Inference Engine:** MYCIN used an inference engine that applied logical reasoning to the rules in the knowledge base. It employed two key methods of reasoning:
   - **Forward Chaining:** Starting with known facts (e.g., patient symptoms or test results) and applying rules to infer new facts.
   - **Backward Chaining:** Working backward from a goal (e.g., a diagnosis) to determine which facts and conditions must be true.
4. **User Interaction:** MYCIN interacted with users, typically doctors or healthcare professionals, by asking a series of questions. These questions were aimed at gathering information about the patient's symptoms, medical history, and lab results. Based on the

answers, MYCIN would evaluate possible diagnoses and recommend appropriate treatments.

5. **Diagnosis and Treatment Recommendations:** After gathering enough information, MYCIN would generate diagnostic suggestions and recommend treatments, including specific antibiotics and dosages. It could also explain the reasoning behind its recommendations, providing users with a justification for the proposed treatment.

Problem Background of the MYCIN Expert System:

diagnosing and treating bacterial illnesses in the 1970s, especially in the area of infectious diseases. Such diseases typically required a thorough examination of the patient's history, lab results, and symptoms, which could be challenging and time-consuming. Additionally, there was a lack of highly qualified specialists, especially in remote or underdeveloped areas where medical professionals might not have been as knowledgeable about particular illnesses. Medical decision-making at the time was primarily based on human judgment, which might be influenced by a variety of factors like fatigue, cognitive overload, and varying levels of experience.This presented a chance to develop an automated system that could offer professional advice and recommendations to help medical professionals make accurate and reliable decisions about diagnosing and treating diseases.

Key Problems Addressed by MYCIN:

1. Complexity of Diagnosing Infectious Diseases: Understanding a range of factors, including as symptoms, test data, and patient history, is necessary to diagnose bacterial infections. It was challenging for physicians, particularly general practitioners, to reliably identify infections due to the large number of possible microorganisms and the wide range of clinical presentations.
2. Lack of Specialists: Many medical personnel lacked sufficient knowledge of infection management due to a lack of infectious disease specialists, especially in rural or underdeveloped locations. In order to make the right diagnostic and treatment decision, general practitioners frequently required assistance.
3. Inconsistent Decision-Making: Depending on a physician's experience, cognitive biases, or busyness, human decision-making in the medical field can vary greatly. Potential inconsistencies in disease management and therapy resulted from the dependence on specialists for each diagnosis.
4. Requirement for Standardized Treatment Protocols: The prescription of antibiotics was frequently determined by empirical judgments rather than by established protocols, which resulted in issues including improper antibiotic administration, inaccurate dosages, or ineffectual therapies. A system that could provide consistent, evidence-based recommendations for treating infections was becoming more and more necessary.

MYCIN's Response to These Problems:

MYCIN was created to overcome these obstacles by simulating human experts' thought processes with AI. MYCIN gave medical professionals automated, evidence-based recommendations for diagnosis and treatment by developing a knowledge base of expert rules and an inference engine that could interpret patient data. This method improved decision-making in the diagnosis and treatment of bacterial infections by lowering diagnostic and therapeutic variability and increasing access to specialized knowledge.

- **CHALLENGES: -**

Despite being revolutionary at the time, the MYCIN expert system encountered a number of difficulties both in its creation and in its possible use. These difficulties stemmed from the restrictions in the expert system's architecture as well as the technology available at the time.

Key Challenges in the MYCIN Expert System:

1.Limited Knowledge Base:

- **Domain-Specific Scope:** Due to its exclusive concentration on bacterial infection diagnosis and treatment, MYCIN had a limited range of applications and was difficult to generalize to other medical specialties. Although sizable for its time, its knowledge base was limited to the particular regulations that specialists provided, and it was difficult to update or grow.
- **Incomplete or Imperfect Knowledge:** Human specialists established the rules that the system followed. The quality and scope of the regulations may limit MYCIN's suggestions because these experts, despite their extensive experience, might not have had perfect or comprehensive understanding.

2.Knowledge Acquisition:

- **Difficulty in Extracting Expertise:** Getting the medical knowledge required to fill MYCIN's knowledge base was one of the main obstacles to its development. Infectious disease specialists were frequently hesitant to codify their expertise into a set of guidelines. Additionally, acquiring information required a significant amount of time and resources.

- **Rule Representation and Maintenance:** MYCIN's rule-based system needed to be updated and revised frequently to maintain its accuracy as medical knowledge advanced. One of the biggest challenges was making sure the regulations kept up with new findings and therapies.

3.Interpretability and Trust:

- **User Trust:** Even though MYCIN was able to suggest diagnosis and treatments, it was not always able to give clear justifications for its conclusions. Users (such as physicians) found it more difficult to trust the system's recommendations because of this lack of transparency, particularly when those recommendations ran counter to their own clinical experience.
- **Expert System Transparency:** Although MYCIN was able to support its suggestions, its users frequently found the reasoning behind its conclusions to be excessively complicated or unclear, particularly in situations involving high stakes in medicine.

4.Inflexibility and Lack of Learning Ability:

- **No Learning from Experience:** MYCIN lacked the capacity to grow over time or learn from fresh data. It was unable to dynamically update its knowledge base in response to new cases or research, unlike contemporary AI systems. The system was static since each update necessitated human interaction to modify the knowledge base.
- **Limited Adaptability:** Due to the rigid definition of MYCIN's regulations, the system found it challenging to adjust to newly discovered illnesses, patient circumstances, or innovative medical discoveries without requiring extensive reprogramming.

MYCIN ARCHITECTURE: -

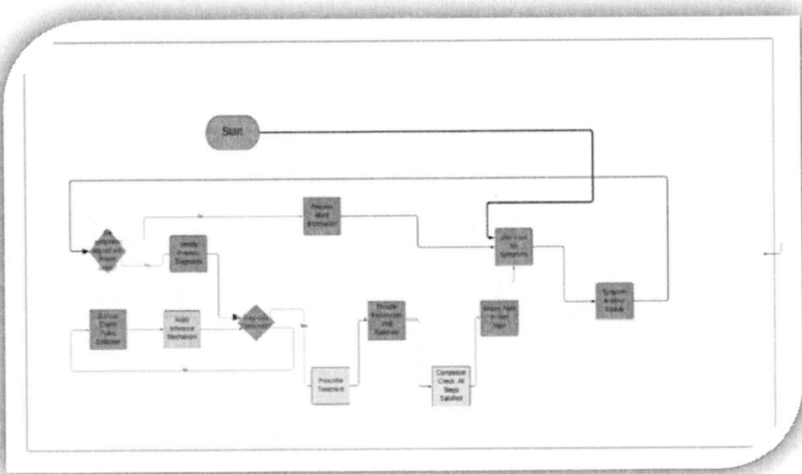

- **LIMITATIONS: -**

1. Narrow Domain of Application
2. Knowledge Base Limitations
3. No Learning or Adaptation
4. User Trust and Acceptance
5. Data Dependency and Quality
6. Limited Explanation of Reasoning
7. Ethical and Legal Concerns
8. Limited Interaction with Users
9. Computational Limitations

Despite being a trailblazing expert system, MYCIN had several drawbacks, such as a limited scope, static knowledge, a dependence on high-quality data, and issues with user trust and flexibility. Due to these restrictions, it was unable to be completely incorporated into actual clinical practice. Notwithstanding these problems, MYCIN was crucial in showcasing AI's potential in medicine and encouraging the creation of increasingly sophisticated healthcare decision-support systems.

- **APPLICATIONS OF MYCIN**

1. **Medical Diagnosis and Decision Support**

One of the earliest AI programs to actively support clinical decision-making was MYCIN. By examining lab findings and patient symptoms, it could:

Determine which germs are causing the infections.

Provide individualized antibiotic regimens that take patient characteristics and medication amounts into account.

The potential for AI to complement human expertise rather than replace it was proved by MYCIN's ability to precisely handle difficult medical issues.

2. **Pioneering Rule-Based Systems**

The information processing "if-then" principles that MYCIN employed were straightforward but efficient. This method demonstrated how structured reasoning might address practical issues and served as a model for developing expert systems in a variety of industries, including manufacturing, banking, and law.

3. **Knowledge Representation and Uncertainty**

A novel feature at the time, MYCIN used certainty criteria to address uncertainty in medical decision-making. This made it possible for the system to deal with ambiguous or missing data, which is still a major obstacle in the development of AI.

4. **A Vision for Personalized Medicine**

MYCIN foreshadowed the concept of customized medicine by customizing diagnosis and treatments for each patient. This idea has been expanded upon by contemporary systems, which use machine learning and massive databases to deliver ever more individualized and complex care.

5. **Educational Tool for Medical Training**

MYCIN was a useful teaching tool in addition to diagnosis. It gave medical students a methodical approach to diagnostic reasoning, motivating them to take into account a variety of variables and methodically evaluate the available data.

6. **Influence on Decision Support Systems**

The success of MYCIN demonstrated how AI may improve human judgment. Today, MYCIN-inspired decision support systems are employed in a variety of sectors, from business analytics to logistics, demonstrating the system's interdisciplinary influence.

7. **A Catalyst for AI Evolution**

The rule-based methodology used by MYCIN was a significant advancement in AI. Hybrid systems that blend machine learning with rule-based reasoning have developed over time, demonstrating how basic concepts can change to address contemporary issues.

- **REVIEW**

MYCIN is unique in the history of artificial intelligence because of its technical accomplishments as well as the insights it provided on the possibilities and difficulties of using AI in practical settings. Examining its advantages and disadvantages in greater detail teaches us important lessons for how we now see AI.

1. **Technical Review**

MYCIN took a novel approach to AI, especially by utilizing a rule-based framework. Expert knowledge becomes easier to update and more accessible by decomposing medical information into precise, well-organized rules. At the time, this was groundbreaking because it showed how AI may democratize access to knowledge. Nevertheless, the system's versatility was limited by its rule-based structure, which was effective for the constrained scope of its activities. MYCIN was less applicable to the more complex and uncertain nature of real-world healthcare since it was unable to adjust to circumstances that deviated from its pre-programmed rules.

Another intriguing aspect was the introduction of assurance factors. It made it possible for MYCIN to "think" about uncertainty, which was difficult to deal with at the time. However, even this advancement had limitations since, in contrast to contemporary AI, which employs more complex techniques to deal with ambiguity and uncertainty, MYCIN's approach to measuring confidence in its responses was crude.

2. **Clinical Impact**

Although MYCIN was never implemented in real hospitals, it had the potential to revolutionize the healthcare industry. In testing, it fared better than general practitioners at identifying bacterial illnesses, especially when there was a lack of immediately available knowledge. This emphasized the system's potential as a tool for enhancing judgment and offering reliable guidance. However, MYCIN was restricted to a single, specific function: the diagnosis of bacterial infections. It was less useful in a real-world clinical setting because of this concentration, which prevented it from handling the entire spectrum of medical disorders that physicians deal with on a regular basis.

3. **Educational Influence**

In addition to its useful applications, MYCIN was important for education. It served as a teaching tool for both computer science and medical students for a long time. They were able to observe firsthand how AI may support reasoning and decision-making. Beyond only serving as a learning aid, MYCIN promoted a cooperative atmosphere where computer scientists and physicians could cooperate to resolve challenging issues. The foundation for the multidisciplinary methods used in contemporary AI research was established by this partnership.

4. **Broader Impact on AI Research**

MYCIN's impact goes much beyond the medical field. It influenced how AI was perceived in terms of knowledge representation and reasoning, and it served as a catalyst for the creation of further expert systems. MYCIN generated new discussions about how robots may mimic—and even improve—human cognition by demonstrating how AI could mimic the decision-making process of human experts. It was a precursor to the idea that AI might find use in industries other than medical, such as finance, law, and customer service.

MYCIN was essentially a ground-breaking technology that showed how AI might support intricate decision-making. Despite its drawbacks, especially with regard to scope and adaptability, it offered important insights into the potential interactions between AI and human expertise. Its legacy serves as a constant reminder of the fine balance between human judgment and machine intelligence, inspiring both the ethical and technical advancement of AI systems.

- **FUTURE SCOPE**

Future developments in AI in healthcare and other fields can be guided by the lessons acquired from MYCIN. Despite MYCIN's limitations at the time, its fundamental concepts might develop into more flexible, user-friendly, and accessible systems that have a significant influence on daily life.

1. **Hybrid AI Models**

Combining contemporary machine learning methods with MYCIN's rule-based methodology is an intriguing prospect for the future. Consider a system that makes judgments based on well-defined rules but also gains insight from data to make better predictions over time. This hybrid strategy could make AI transparent and flexible while striking a compromise between machine learning's flexibility and human-like thinking. This might be particularly helpful in the healthcare industry, where real-time patient data and structured expert knowledge are essential.

2. **Personalized Medicine**

MYCIN-inspired systems may also develop in the field of personalized healthcare. AI could assist in developing individualized treatment strategies by considering a patient's genetic composition, lifestyle, and environmental factors in addition to their symptoms. MYCIN's foundation of offering tailored treatment recommendations might be extended to include a greater range of medical issues, bringing it closer to the goal of precision medicine. This trend toward customized medicine is already under progress.

3. **Explainable AI**

Making sure that systems are accountable and comprehensible is one of the main challenges in contemporary AI. By outlining the logic underlying its diagnosis, MYCIN made a first step in this approach, but we may go farther by increasing the transparency of AI. The goal of AI in the future is probably going to be to make complicated models not just accurate but also understandable to people. In the healthcare industry, where professionals must comprehend and have faith in the system's judgments, this will be essential. Physicians are more willing to use AI as a tool in their daily work if it can clearly explain its reasons.

4. **Global Healthcare Applications**

MYCIN-inspired AI systems may also make a significant difference in places with scarce healthcare resources. Imagine a doctor in a far-off village utilizing a tablet or smartphone to diagnose and treat patients with the help of artificial intelligence. We could provide expert-level medical consultations anywhere in the globe by incorporating AI into telemedicine, which would help close the disparities in access to healthcare. In low-resource settings, where there are frequently few qualified medical personnel, these methods could be quite helpful.

5. **Real-Time Decision Making**

Real-time decision-making is another area where AI has potential for the future. Smart health trackers and wearable technology, for instance, are getting increasingly advanced and are collecting a multitude of information on a person's health. AI might incorporate this data into a system that offers real-time guidance or notifications, possibly identifying health problems before they become serious. With AI acting as a proactive, ongoing support system, this could revolutionize the way that patients and doctors communicate.

6. **Integration with Emerging Technologies**

The potential for MYCIN-inspired systems is limitless as emerging technologies like natural language processing (NLP) and the Internet of Things (IoT) advance. While IoT devices might immediately input real-time data from wearables and sensors into diagnostic systems, natural language processing (NLP) could enable AI to evaluate medical literature or even patient chats. By combining these technologies, AI might become more than just a tool for decision assistance; it could become an active player in the healthcare ecosystem, providing more accurate insights based on data.

REFERENCES

1.Shortliffe, E. H. (1976). Computer-Based Medical Consultations: MYCIN. Elsevier.

2. Buchanan, B. G., &Shortliffe, E. H. (1984). Rule-Based Expert Systems: The MYCIN Experiments of the Stanford Heuristic Programming Project. Addison-Wesley.

3. Nilsson, N. J. (1998). Artificial Intelligence: A New Synthesis. Morgan Kaufmann.

5. Miller, T. (2019). “Explanation in Artificial Intelligence: Insights from the Social Sciences.” Artificial Intelligence, 267, 1-38.
6. Amodei, D., et al. (2016). “Concrete Problems in AI Safety.” arXiv preprint arXiv:1606.06565.
7. Gorry, G. A., & Barnett, G. O. (1968). “Experience with a Model of Sequential Diagnosis.” Computers and Biomedical Research, 1(5), 490-507.
8. Clancey, W. J. (1983). “The Epistemology of a Rule-Based Expert System—A Framework for Explanation.” Artificial Intelligence, 20(3), 215-251.
9. Topol, E. J. (2019). Deep Medicine: How Artificial Intelligence Can Make Healthcare Human Again. Basic Books.

10. https://www.ijresm.com/Vol_1_2018/Vol1_Iss9_September18/IJRESM_19_22.pdf?utm_source=chatgpt.com

Impact of Blended Learning Strategies on Concept Attainment

Mudasir Amin
Assistant Professor Akal University Talwandi Sabo Bathinda-Punjab India
E-mail: mudasiramin861@gmail.com

Abstract

The learner is the epitome of the entire teaching learning process. While teaching in the classrooms, one comes across different types of learners under one roof. It is said that "No two individuals are alike." Thus, it demands blended learning technique of teaching that caters to the needs of all the types of individuals.The blended Learning has become an important method in education system in this century generally and particularly in commerce, and management subjects.The study examined the Blended learning as a strategy for obtaining the cognition and concepts based on the active learning. The study adopted the quasi-experimental research design. The results indicated that blended learning strategies had a positive impact on concept attainment of Graduate students. By effectively blending online learning with face-to-face instruction, concept attainment ability of students can be improved. Blended learning strategies can be considered as one of the new initiatives of pedagogical approaches for integrating technology in education system. It is presumed that blended learning strategies would yield fruitful results in the hands of resourceful persons, experts, administrators, curriculum planners and educators who have a positive blend for making transformative changes in the teaching learning process.

Keywords: Blended Learning, Concept Attainment, Learning Process, Graduate students.

1. INTRODUCTION

The vast and explosive scientific and technological revolution has produced a fantastic growth of scientific knowledge in most fields of human activity. As a result the education system is confronted with pressure to adapt educational programs that reflect new ways of learning. It is essential to provide a variety of strategies for maximizing learning of heterogeneous group of learners. Some of the most effective establishments are using dynamic digital tools such as e-Learning along with traditional classroom practices to create blended learning models. In order to prepare lifelong learners of the 21st century concept attainment is important. Concept attainment is the process of defining a big idea by attending to its essential attributes, distinguishing them from associated attributes that are not essential to the meaning.

The rapid advancement of digital technology has significantly transformed the landscape of education, leading to the emergence of innovative teaching and learning methodologies. Among these, blended learning—a pedagogical approach that combines traditional face-to-face classroom instruction with online learning experiences—has gained prominence for its ability to create flexible, interactive, and student-centered learning environments. In recent years, educators have increasingly adopted blended learning strategies to enhance student engagement, accommodate diverse learning styles, and improve academic outcomes. One crucial aspect of student learning is concept attainment, which refers to the process through which learners acquire, understand, and apply key concepts within a subject area. Effective concept attainment not only strengthens cognitive understanding but also fosters critical thinking and problem-solving abilities. Since traditional teaching methods often rely on rote memorization and linear instruction, they may not fully address the varied needs of learners in conceptual understanding. Blended learning strategies, by integrating multimedia resources, collaborative tools, and self-paced learning opportunities with classroom interaction, hold the potential to bridge this gap. Therefore, investigating the impact of blended learning strategies on concept attainment is essential for understanding how this approach influences learners' comprehension, retention, and application of knowledge, and how it can be leveraged to improve the overall quality of education in contemporary classrooms.

1.1 Concept of Blended Learning

The term Blended Learning was initially used in 1997 in U.K. According to **Spanier (2002)**, "It is the largest unknown trend in higher education." Blended learning is an innovative concept that integrates innovative and technological advances of online learning with interaction and participation of traditional classroom teaching.

Garrison and **Vaughan (2008)** mentioned blended learning as "the thoughtful fusion of face-to-face and online learning experiences" emphasizing the need for reflection on traditional approaches and for redesigning learning and teaching in this new terrain.

While **Carter (2009)** stated blended learning as a strategic and considered approach to teaching and learning that effectively integrates different models of teaching and styles of learning whereby both face-to-face and online learning are each made better by the presence of the other.

1.2 Concept of Concept Attainment

A concept is the basic unit of all types of learning. Concepts permeate the cognitive process and serve as organizers of all intellectual and cognitive activities. Concept attainment is a structured inquiry process to help bring meaning to new concepts by highlighting similarities and differences. **Joyce** and **Weil (1967)** said that concept attainment, a close relative to inductive thinking, focuses on the decision-making and categorization processes leading up to the creation and understanding of a concept.

Joyce et al (2014) expressed that concept attainment processes structured inquiry through positive examples (exemplars) that provide characteristics, properties and attributes which are distinctive to a concept and negative examples (non-exemplars) as clues which help eliminate characteristics that do not apply to the concept.

2. REVIEW OF RELATED LITERATURE

Literature snapshot on the "Impact of Blended Learning Strategies on Concept Attainment," emphasizing what's known, how it was studied, and where gaps remain—especially in the Indian context:**Harris, Hall, Muirhead, McAteer, Schmoller**and **Thorpe (2004)** conducted a study on the impact of e-Learning on learners' participation, attainment, retention and progression in further education. The results indicated that key informants were positive about the effect of e-Learning on participation, retention and attainment with potential impact thought to occur by: creating a sense of engagement, excitement and involvement, the personalization of the learning interface to individual needs and by improving communication.**Kumar (2010)** carried out an experimental study on effect of the blended strategies on learning retention and attitude of secondary school students. The findings of the study revealed that students taught through blended learning retained the learning material significantly for longer time than the students taught through traditional methods.**Nazarenko (2015)** carried out a comparative study of blended learning vs. traditional learning (a case study). Majority of the students (96%) were positive about the blended format of the course.**Kariyana**and**Sonn (2017)** assessed the relationship between teaching methods and learners' concept formation, development and integration in geometry. The paper recommends ways to improve classroom practices arguing that an omission or poor development of one learning stage will heinously affect the proper development of all the succeeding stages.**Nouby**and **Alkhazali (2017)** studied the effect of designing a blended learning environment on achievement and deep learning of graduate students at the Arabian Gulf University. The results showed that the scores on post application of achievement scores and deep learning scale were improved.**Paul** and **Richard (2017)** carried out a study on the effect of blended learning approach on students' academic achievement and retention: A case study of Air Force Secondary School River State, Nigeria. The results indicated that students taught using blended learning performed more and have higher retention than students taught by conventional method.Direct evidence on concept attainment within blended settings is emerging but still sparse.**Ministry of Education Reports (2020–2023)** emphasized blended learning in alignment with NEP-2020 and noted both opportunities and challenges in the Indian context. The reports underline that infrastructure gaps, teacher preparation, and coherent design strongly influence the success of blended learning in fostering conceptual learning.**Maharjan (2022)** carried out a quasi-experimental study with Grade 9 science learners and demonstrated that students exposed to blended learning achieved higher test scores and developed more positive attitudes towards science learning than those in traditional classrooms, indirectly supporting blended learning's role in conceptual growth.**Zhang and Li (2023)** through a meta-analysis of blended learning studies across multiple countries, concluded that blended learning generally improves student performance, attitudes, and achievement. While not specific to concept attainment, the findings indicate that blended environments foster conditions conducive to deep conceptual understanding.**Singh and Kaur (2024)** proposed and tested a Constructivist Concept Attainment Model (CCAM) with Grade 9 students in Punjab, India. Their study employed a randomized pre-test/post-test design and revealed that students in the CCAM group achieved significantly higher concept acquisition in Social Studies compared to lecture-based controls, suggesting the model's strong effectiveness in enhancing conceptual learning in a blended environment.**Rani et al. (2024)** conducted an experimental study in elementary Social Studies and found that integrating the Concept Attainment Model into blended learning significantly improved students' ability to acquire and classify concepts compared to traditional methods, highlighting the model's applicability in hybrid classrooms.**Khan et al. (2024)** found that blended learning interventions in Indian higher education improved not only academic achievement but also student readiness and motivation, both of which are important for successful concept integration and attainment.**Patel and Sharma (2025)** using qualitative approaches, reported that technological scaffolds embedded in blended learning encouraged collaborative knowledge construction and critical thinking, which are precursors to effective concept attainment.

WHAT'S THE CONSENSUS AND THE GAP?

Together, the evidence suggests that blended learning—especially when paired with explicit concept-attainment routines (e.g., Bruner's examples/non-examples, hypothesis testing, immediate feedback)—can significantly enhance concept acquisition. However, there are few rigorous, large-sample studies that directly measure "concept attainment" as the outcome within blended environments, particularly in Indian K-12 contexts. More randomized or well-matched quasi-experimental studies that (a) operationalize concept attainment with validated tools and (b) detail the blended design features (LMS workflows, feedback cadence, sequencing of online vs. face-to-face concept tasks) are still needed.

3. JUSTIFICATION OF THE STUDY

In the past, the organization of learning was largely teacher-controlled, with instructors directing content delivery, pacing, and assessment; however, the rapid scientific and technological revolutions of recent decades have shifted the educational paradigm from rote memorization toward active knowledge construction. This shift demands greater emphasis on learning modes that promote self-regulation, metacognition, and authentic application of knowledge rather than passive reception of facts. Blended learning—an intentional combination of face-to-face instruction and digital learning experiences—embodies this shift by offering flexible, learner-centered opportunities for interaction, reflection, and collaboration; it encourages students to engage with material at their own pace, to seek out resources, and to participate in meaningful problem solving. Concepts function as the "furniture" of the mind: they organize experience, enable transfer, and form the scaffolding on which new learning is built. Meaningful learning therefore requires that new information be integrated into learners' existing conceptual schemas; absent such integration, instruction tends toward superficial or rote retention that fails to support deep understanding or application. Concept-attainment strategies—structured approaches that help learners discriminate defining attributes of categories and test hypotheses about category membership—support this integrative process by guiding students to identify which features are essential, which are incidental, and which do not belong, thereby strengthening both conceptual clarity and transfer. Although international literature indicates promising links between blended instructional designs and higher-order learning outcomes, relatively few empirical studies have investigated the specific effects of blended learning on concept attainment within the Indian educational context, and even fewer have examined how concept-attainment techniques perform when embedded in blended environments. This gap highlights the need for focused research to determine how blended modalities and concept-attainment strategies can be combined most effectively to foster conceptual understanding, critical thinking, and sustained learning in contemporary classrooms.

4. OPERATIONAL DEFINITIONS OF THE TERMS USED

Blended Learning Strategies

Blended learning is an innovative approach to teaching which combines the best elements of online and face-to-face education. In the present study the blended learning strategies meant use of MS Word documents, ppt's, audio clippings, video clippings and online test components, online discussions rightly blended with face-to-face components to make blended learning application module.

Concept Attainment

A concept is the basic unit of all types of learning. Concept attainment refers to the state of having achieved a concept, the terminal point of concept formation. In the present study concept attainment referred to attainment of concepts of social science by students as reflected through the scores of concept attainment ability test selected by the investigator.

5. OBJECTIVES OF THE STUDY

1. To study the impact of blended learning on concept attainment of graduate students.
2. To find out the difference in scores of concept attainment of experimental and control group on pre-test.
3. To find out the difference in scores of concept attainment of control group on pre-test and post-test.
4. To find out the difference in scores of concept attainment of experimental group on pre-test and post-test.
5. To find out the difference in scores of concept attainment of experimental and control group on post-test.
6. To suggest some educational implications based on outcomes of the study.

6. HYPOTHESES OF THE STUDY

There is no significant difference in scores of concept attainment of experimental and control group on pre-test.

There is no significant difference in scores of concept attainment of control group on pre-test and post-test.

There is no significant difference in scores of concept attainment of experimental group on pre-test and post-test.

There is no significant difference in scores of concept attainment of experimental and control group on post-test.

7. RESEARCH METHODOLOGY AND PROCEDURE

For the present researchthe quasi-experimental research design was used. Pre-test on concept attainment was administered to both the control group and the experimental group. Then the experimental group was taught using blended learning strategies and the control group was taught using conventional method. After that the post test was administered to both the groups.For the present study the students studying at graduate level constituted the population. The sample consists of 360 graduate students, 180 in experimental group and 180 in control group.In this research in order to measure the concept attainment ability, the Concept Attainment Test (CAT) was used. The results were analyzed and interpreted by using t-test.

8. ANALYSIS AND INTERPRETATION OF RESULTS

Hypothesis 1

Group	N	Mean	S.D	r	t-value	Level of Significance
Experimental Group	180	16	3.45	-0.14	0.51	NotSignificantat 0.05 level
Control Group	180	15.28	4.27			

Table A showing result of t-test for experimental group and control group on pretest

Interpretation: From the table it can be interpreted that the calculated value of t is 0.51 which is less than 1.96 at 0.05 level of significance.Hence the hypothesis no. 1 stating, "There is no significant difference in scores of concept attainment of experimental and control group on pre-test" is accepted at said level.

Hypothesis 2

Group	N	Mean	S.D	r	t-value	Level of Significance
Control Group	180	15.28	4.27	0.307	0.52	NotSignificantat 0.05 level
ControlGroup	180	15.94	4.59			

Table B showing result of t-test for control group on pretest and post test

Interpretation: From the table B it can be interpreted that the calculated value of t is 0.52 which is less than 1.96 at 0.05 level of significance.Hence the hypothesis no. 2 stating, "There is no significant difference in scores of concept attainment of control group on pre-test and post-test" is accepted at said level.

Hypothesis 3

Group	N	Mean	S.D	r	t-value	Level of Significance
ExperimentalGroup	180	16	3.45	0.60	3.60	Significantat0.01 level
ExperimentalGroup	180	20.28	6.09			

Table C showing result of t-test for experimental group on pre-test and post-test

Interpretation: From the table C it can be interpreted that the calculated value of t is 3.60 which is more than 2.57 at 0.01 level of significance.Hence the hypothesis no. 3 stating, "There is no significant difference in scores of concept attainment of experimental group on pre-test and post-test" is rejected at said level.

Hypothesis 4

Group	N	Mean	S.D	r	t-value	Level of Significance
Experimental Group	180	20.28	6.09	-0.02	2.32	Significantat0.01 level
Control Group	180	15.94	4.59			

Table D showing result of t-test for experimental and control group on post test

Interpretation: From the table D it can be interpreted that the calculated value of t is 2.32 which is more than 1.96 at 0.05 level of significance.Hence the hypothesis no. 4 stating, "There is no significant difference in scores of concept attainment of experimental and control group on post-test" is rejected at said level.

9. GENERAL FINDINGS

- There was no significant difference in scores of concept attainment of experimental and control group on pre-test.
- There was no significant difference in scores of concept attainment of control group on pre-test and post-test.
- There was significant difference in scores of concept attainment of experimental group on pre-test and post-test.
- There was significant difference in scores of concept attainment of experimental and control group on post-test.

10. EDUCATIONAL IMPLICATIONS

The study presents a model of integrating online learning with face-to-face teaching at tertiary level.The study highlights positive effects of blended learning strategies over conventional approach in developing concept attainment ability.The present research has implications on framing Government policies to improve quality of learning by integrating technology in education system.The study may initiate discussions in educational sector for evolving new initiatives in pedagogical approach to empower students so as to become life-long learners of 21st century.By recognizing and carefully balancing the learners' needs, preferred or common learning methods and the available resources, blended learning provides a significant increase in the effectiveness of learning, bringing a greater experience facilitating activities and helping to transform theory into practice.The study recommends that blended learning provides a platform for close interaction between the learner and the subject matter in supportive manner. The students can learn the basic concepts in an effective manner. It is presumed that blended learning strategies would yield fruitful results in the hands of resourceful persons, experts, administrators, curriculum planners and educators who have a positive blend for making transformative changes in the teaching learning process.

An outcome of the study is that the experimental group using blended learning strategies attained higher scores in concept attainment than the control group taught using traditional method. The reason of such an outcome may be that blended learning approach ensures that the learner is engaged to provide unique learning styles that help them in attaining the concepts.

11. CONCLUSION

The study was an attempt to find the effect of blended learning strategies on concept attainment of graduate students. The study revealed that blended learning strategies had a positive impact on concept attainment of students. By effectively blending online learning with face-to-face instruction, concept attainment ability of students can be improved. Blended learning strategies can be considered as one of the new initiatives of pedagogical approaches for integrating technology in education. It is presumed that blended learning strategies would yield fruitful results in the hands of resourceful persons, experts, administrators, curriculum planners and educators who have a positive blend for making transformative changes in the teaching learning process.

REFERENCES

Battye, G., & Carter, H. (2009). Report on the review of online and blended learning. Canberra, ACT:
University of Canberra (Retrieved June 25, 2012, from http://www.canberra.edu.au/tlc/attachments/pdf/OBLR_FINAL-JUN09.pdf)

Garrison, D. R., & Vaughan, N. D. (2008). Blended learning in higher education: Framework, principles,
and guidelines. The Jossey-Bass higher and adult education series. San Francisco: Jossey-Bass.

Harris, R., Hall, J., Muirhead, A., McAteer, E., Schmoller, S., & Thorpe, G. (2004). Impact of e-learning
on learner participation, attainment, retention, and progression in further education: Report of a scoping study. Glasgow, UK: Scottish Centre for Research into On-Line Learning & Assessment, University of Glasgow.

Joyce Bruce and Weil Marsha (1967).Models of Teaching.Prentice Hall of India Pvt. Ltd. New Delhi.

Joyce, B., Weil, M., & Calhoun, E. (2014). Models of teaching (9th ed.). Boston: Pearson Education, Inc.

Kariyana and Sonn (2017).Teaching Methods and Learners' Concept Formation, Development and
Integration in Geometry: Assessing the Relationship. International Journal of Educational Sciences, 12(1), 75-88. DOI:10.1080/09751122.2016.11890415

Kumar, P. (2010). An experimental study of the effect of blended learning strategies on learning retention
and attitude of secondary school students (Unpublished Doctoral Thesis.Chaudhary Charan Singh University.Shodhganga.http://hdl.handle.net/10603/21927

Nazarenko, A. L. (2015). Blended learning vs. traditional learning: What works?(A case study research).
Procedia-Social and Behavioral Sciences, 200, 77-82. DOI:10.1016/J.SBSPRO.2015.08.018

Nouby&Alkhazali (2017).The Effect of Designing a Blended Learning Environment on Achievement
and Deep Learning of Graduate Students at the Arabian Gulf University. Open Journal of Social Sciences. 05(10), 248-260. DOI: 10.4236/jss.2017.510022

Paul & Richard (2017).Blended learning approach on students' academic achievement and retention: A
case study of air force secondary school rivers state, Nigeria. International Journal of Multidisciplinary Research and Development, 4(12), 15-21.

Ministry of Education. (2020–2023). Reports on blended learning implementation under NEP-2020.Government of India, New Delhi.
Maharjan, P. (2022). Blended learning and science achievement: A quasi-experimental study of grade nine learners. International Journal of Science Education, 44(6), 789–804.
Zhang, Y., & Li, H. (2023). A meta-analysis of blended learning outcomes: Performance, attitudes, and achievement. Educational Research Review, 38, 100–124.
Khan, R., Ahmed, S., &Bano, T. (2024). Blended learning interventions in Indian higher education: Effects on achievement and motivation. Journal of Educational Technology Research, 12(3), 45–58.
Rani, P., Verma, A., & Gupta, K. (2024). Concept attainment model in blended learning: An experimental study in Social Studies classrooms. Elementary Education Review, 8(2), 101–115.
Singh, H., & Kaur, J. (2024). Constructivist Concept Attainment Model: An experimental study on social studies learning. Indian Journal of Educational Research, 18(1), 56–70.
Patel, M., & Sharma, R. (2025). Technological scaffolds and knowledge construction in blended classrooms: A qualitative study. Asian Journal of Education and Development, 17(1), 21–36.

WEB REFERENCES

http://en.wikibooks.org/wiki/Blended_Learning_in_K-12/The_many_names_of_Blended_Learning

AI Agents Streamline Automation, Detect Anomalies, and Forecast Economic Outcomes

Dr. S. Govardhan[1], Dr. R. Sureka[2],
[1]Associate Professor, Department of Business Administration,
sgovardhanmba@gmail.com
St. Mary's Group of Institutions Hyderabad
[2]Assistant Professor, Department of Business Administration, CHENNAIS AMRITA IIHM

Abstract:
Artificial intelligence (AI) agents are revolutionizing decision-making and operations across various fields by automating repetitive tasks, increasing efficiency, and optimizing resource utilization. They excel at anomaly detection, mitigating risks such as financial misuse, manufacturing defects, and cyber threats, thereby enhancing resilience. AI-powered forecasting models analyze vast datasets to predict economic events, enabling organizations and policymakers to plan for market changes, evaluate investments, and strategize for sustainable growth. The combined capabilities of automation, anomaly detection, and economic forecasting demonstrate the versatility of AI agents in tackling real-world complexity, fostering efficient operations, proactive risk management, and data-driven intelligence. As industries increasingly adopt intelligent systems, AI agents are poised to be crucial in shaping future economies, promoting resilient, adaptive, and innovation-driven environments.
Keywords: Defects, Cyber Threats, Enabling, Complexity, Proactive, Resilient

1.0 Introduction:

AI agents are also radically changing the manner companies conduct their operations by uniting intelligence and automation. Such systems automate ordinary tasks, but also introduce flexibility and efficiency in challenging decision making. AI agents are more efficient as an automated model can perform repetitive tasks and minimize mistakes. Due to their superior algorithms, they can identify anomalies in data early in advance, so actions can be taken to prevent any risk and inefficiencies before they arise. AI-based forecasting offers new opportunities to get to know economic dynamics, which enables enterprises and governments to make predictions and overcome adversity. In sum, such abilities point to the centrality of AI agents in the development of intelligent, robust, and future-proof systems.

The Triple Bottom Line (TBL) model proposes to extend the traditional focus on the financial bottom line, to a triple bottom line that also include an environmental bottom line and a social bottom line. It stresses on three major pillars, which are People, Planet, and Profit. Improvements in the People dimension focus on social responsibility, decent work practices and community welfare. Planet emphasizes ecological sustainability, effective utilization of resources and limited impact on the environment. The term profit refers to an economic value addition and company development. Balance combination of the three aspects helps the TBL framework prompt business organizations and institutions to be sustainable in the long run. It informs ethical decision-making, and environmental sustainability, a
nd cost-viability, which lies in ensuring that it creates value to its stakeholders and the society.

1.1 The Changing Business Landscape:

During the 20th century, profit and shareholder wealth constituted the principal measures of corporate growth. The 20 th century however has placed the emphasis on triple bottom line: People, Planet and Profit. More and more it is required that companies contribute to investors by returning on investments and that companies respond in areas such as climatic change, resource shortage and inequality. Two of the prominent fields in the change include Sustainable Finance and Green Marketing. They collectively assist organizations in the responsible expansion that can be branded as a mixture of economic prosperity and environmental and social impact.

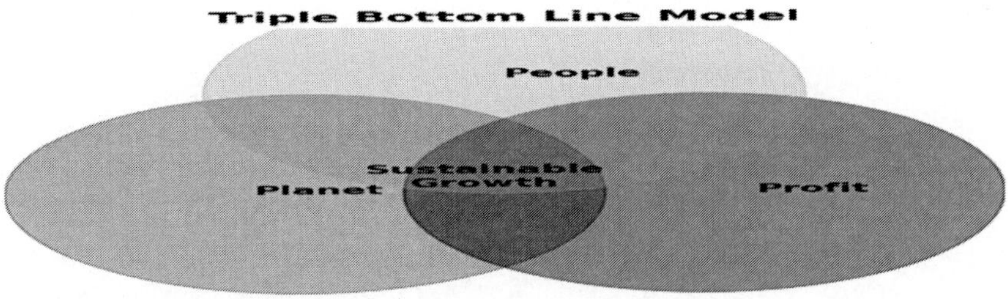

1.2 Sustainable Finance and Green Marketing:

Sustainable Finance can be defined as the practice of financial decision-making using an Environmental, social and governance (ESG) criteria. This includes: Investments in social enterprises, renewable energy and clean technologies. Financial instruments such as green bonds, carbon credits and impact funds. Risk management strategies that factor climate risks and changes in regulations. In plain language, a Sustainable Finance is a process that makes capital flow to business projects that are beneficial to society. Green Marketing is the creation of designing, promoting and delivering products or services that are nature-friendly. It devotes attention to environmentally friendly packaging and designing of sustainable products as well, to avoid green washing, honest communication is needed. Establishing consumer credibility on bridge. Lepretranaivordina prioritizing transparency Green Marketing does not only mean promoting a product--it means creating a brand story that conveys care of the earth and sustainability.

1.3 Rationale of a dual approach and World trends:

Finance and marketing are functions that are not kept in the same way. Finance observes numbers, returns and risk; marketing is concerned with customers, branding and industry engagement. But the challenge of sustainability requires integration. **For example:** Green Bond issued to fund a renewable energy plant will not succeed unless the customers would take the renewable energy solutions. In a similar way, a green marketing campaign can also fail in case it is not economically viable or cannot be based on sustainable investing. Therefore, finance gives the resources foundation and marketing makes the change of behavior and acceptance in the market. Customers are selecting the brands that are showing sustainability. Pressure by investors: Investors are increasingly investing in ESG compliant portfolios. Regulations: Governments and institutions are dictating the need to report on sustainability. Specific tools: Digital tools, AI, and blockchain are boosting transparency both in the world of finance and the world of marketing.

2.1 Theories and Frameworks in Sustainable Business:

The integration of sustainability into business practice is influenced by key theories like the Triple Bottom Line (TBL) and Environmental, Social, and Governance (ESG) principles, alongside the stakeholder vs. shareholder debate. The TBL framework, as defined by John Elkington, expands business success beyond profit to include social and environmental dimensions, aiming for equilibrium between economic returns, community development, and ecological care for sustainable growth. ESG principles serve as a tool for investors, regulators, and companies to measure non-financial performance, assessing resource efficiency, carbon emissions, and energy use (Environmental); labor practices, diversity, and community engagement (Social); and ethical leadership, transparency, and board responsibility (Governance). ESG has become a universal standard for sustainable finance, linking corporate actions to long-term risk analysis and value creation.

2.2 Growth of Global Sustainable Investment:

Very much related to these theses is the debate of stakeholder and shareholder points of view. Shareholder view lays stress on the investor-owner returns, which mostly focuses on short-term earnings. Conversely, in stakeholder approach businesses are understood to work as part of a bigger chain which involves the employees, consumers, the suppliers, governments and the society in general. Sustainable strategies will involve companies to factor in the interest of the various groups of people so that integrity in profitability is seen to be attained without compromising ethical or environmental concerns. Altogether, the two frameworks can serve as a multifaceted approach to incorporating the concept of sustainability into organizational processes, making sure that organizations manage to build a competitive environment while taking care of the welfare of the society and the planet.

Sources: Elkington, J. (1997). Cannibals with Forks: The Triple Bottom Line of 21st Century Business. Capstone Publishing.Freeman, R. E. (1984). Strategic Management: A Stakeholder Approach. Pitman Publishing.

Table 1: Growth of Global Sustainable Investment (2020–2022)

Year	Global Sustainable Investment (USD Trillion)	% of Total Managed Assets
2020	35.3	36%
2022	41.0	39%

Interpretation: Global sustainable investment rose from USD 35.3 trillion in 2020 to USD 41 trillion in 2022, indicating investor confidence in ESG-driven finance. The share of total assets managed sustainably continues to grow, highlighting mainstream adoption.

2..3 Consumer Preference

Table 2: Consumer Preference for Eco-Friendly Products (2021–2023)

Year	Consumers Preferring Sustainable Brands (%)	Increase from Previous Survey
2021	58%	—
2023	72%	+14%

Interpretation: Eco-conscious consumerism shows strong momentum, with preference for sustainable brands rising from 58% in 2021 to 72% in 2023. The growth signals increasing trust in green marketing, with businesses compelled to integrate sustainability into core branding strategies.

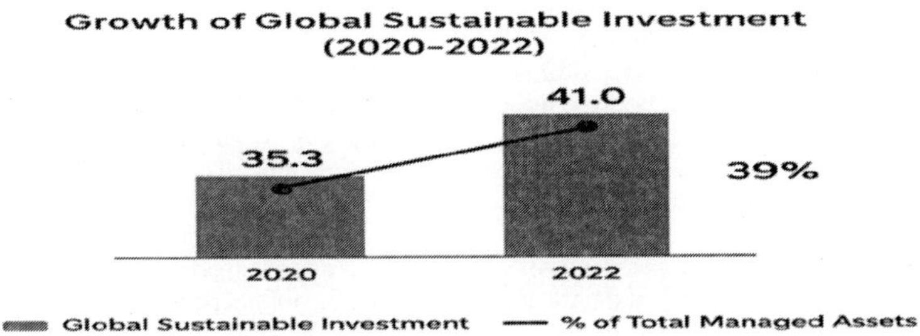

3.1 Principles of Sustainable Finance:

Sustainable finance integrates environmental, social, and governance (ESG) factors into investment and fundraising to align financial goals with long-term societal and environmental objectives. This approach is underpinned by responsible investment strategies, which include ESG screening for resilience and value, and Socially Responsible Investment (SRI) that favors ethical industries. Impact investing specifically targets positive social and environmental returns alongside financial gains, promoting sustainable development. The framework also utilizes green financial instruments such as green bonds for projects like renewable energy, carbon credits to incentivize emission reductions, and climate finance to support climate adaptation and mitigation in vulnerable economies. Furthermore, sustainable finance acknowledges and incorporates sustainability-related risks, such as those arising from resource scarcity and climate change, into financial risk assessment models to enhance institutional resilience.

3.2. Measuring and Reporting Sustainability in Finance:

To integrate sustainability into the financial system, accurate measurement and transparent reporting are essential for stakeholders to assess corporate sustainability. International standards, amalgamated systems, and assessment indices aim to enhance comparability and accountability. Key reporting frameworks include the Global Reporting Initiative (GRI) for broad indicators and the Sustainability Accounting Standard Board (SASB) for sector-specific financial materiality. The International Sustainability Standards Board (ISSB) is developing global standards to create a consistent reporting model. Integrated reporting combines financial and non-financial information to show how sustainability drives value. Disclosures on climate-related financial risk, particularly following the Task Force on Climate-related Financial Disclosures (TCFD) recommendations, are becoming globally mandatory. Tools like ESG ratings and sustainable indices (e.g., Dow Jones Sustainability Index, FTSE4Good) measure corporate actions in environmental stewardship, social responsibility, and governance, guiding capital and encouraging sustainability, despite rating inconsistencies.

3.3 Methodology:

This book employs a multi-disciplinary and exploratory methodology, integrating finance, marketing, sustainability, and policy studies. The research design combines secondary and conceptual analysis to balance theory, practice, and new knowledge. Secondary sources include peer-reviewed journals, books, and reports from global agencies (UN, World Bank, EU), as well as industry white papers, systematically analyzed for common patterns, theoretical frameworks, and trends in sustainable finance and green marketing. While prioritizing sources published within the last ten years for current relevance, foundational works on stakeholder theory and the triple bottom line were included for conceptual depth. A comparative model was used to examine sustainability practices in developed and emerging economies, with case studies selected for relevancy, replicability, and practical significance, highlighting both successful implementations and lessons from failures. The analysis covers financial and marketing concepts such as ESG, SRI, green bonds, and climate finance, alongside marketing strategies like eco-branding, green consumer behavior, and digital sustainability campaigns. To ensure objectivity, diverse perspectives from academia, regulatory bodies, corporate leadership, and consumer research were incorporated. Visual aids, including models and diagrams, were utilized to enhance clarity for academic readers, practitioners, and policymakers. This approach provides a structured yet flexible framework to bridge theory and practice, emphasizing the interdependencies between finance and marketing in fostering responsible growth.

3.4 Table 3: Global Green Bond Issuance (2020–2023)

Year	Green Bond Issuance (USD Billion)	Annual Growth (%)
2020	297	—
2021	522	+76%
2022	487	-7%
2023	575	+18%

Interpretation: Green bond issuance surged from USD 297 billion in 2020 to USD 575 billion in 2023, despite a dip in 2022. The overall growth reflects investor demand for climate finance instruments to support sustainable infrastructure and renewable projects.

Table 4: Renewable Energy Share in Global Power Generation (2020–2023)

Year	Renewable Share (%)	Increase from Previous Year
2020	28%	—
2021	29.5%	+1.5%
2022	30.6%	+1.1%
2023	32.0%	+1.4%

Interpretation: The renewable share in global power generation steadily rose from 28% in 2020 to 32% in 2023. This upward trend demonstrates accelerating adoption of clean energy technologies, driven by policy mandates, cost reductions, and global commitments to net-zero targets.

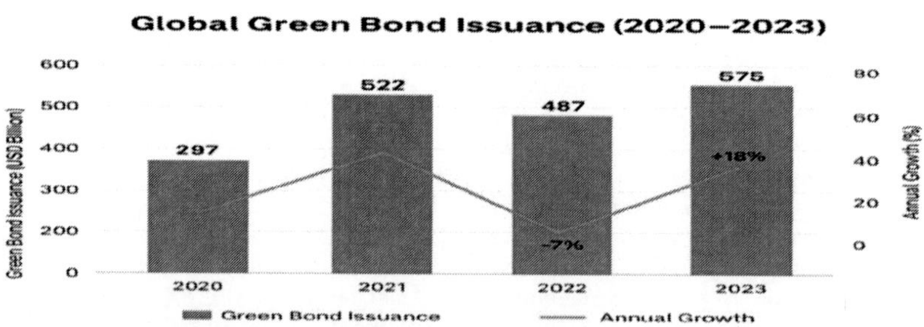

3.4. Case Studies in Sustainable Finance

Concrete case studies illustrate the practical application of sustainable financial concepts, detailing the roles of banks, investors, and regulators. Analysis of these examples, such as Apple's green bond for renewable energy and the World Bank's financing of development projects, demonstrates the impact of financial innovation on environmental and social outcomes. Tesla's model integrates various financing methods to embed environmental goals into capital deployment. Banks like Yes Bank and the State Bank of India are issuing green bonds and sustainable loans for renewable energy. Growing investor interest in responsible decision-making elevates the importance of ESG ratings and sustainability indices. Regulators are encouraged to implement disclosure standards and promote low-carbon initiatives, drawing from European and Asian market practices. The success of sustainable finance relies on collaboration through clear reporting, innovative instruments, and engagement from all stakeholders. Emerging markets can adopt international experiences to integrate sustainability into financial decision-making, fostering responsible growth.

Source: Scholtens, B. (2006). "Finance as a Driver of Corporate Social Responsibility." Journal of Business Ethics, 68(1), 19–33.Flammer, C. (2021). "Corporate Green Bonds." Journal of Financial Economics, 142(2), 499–516.

Green Marketing

4.1 Green Consumer Behavior

Businesses seeking to align marketing with sustainability must understand green consumer behavior. Green consumers prioritize environmental and ethical practices, influenced by values, responsibility, and social norms, favoring products with minimal impact and those supporting social causes. Segmentation based on demographics, lifestyle, or willingness to pay a premium allows for effective targeting. Early adopters of green technologies are a high-influence segment that sets market trends, and businesses can optimize adoption and loyalty by tailoring communications, pricing, and distribution. Consumer trust, built through transparency, certifications, and substantiated claims, is critical, as greenwashing erodes credibility. Authentic, consistent communication, validated independently, fosters trust and enduring sustainable practices. Green consumer behavior is a complex interplay of psychological drivers, marketing, and trust management, and businesses that integrate this understanding can cultivate loyalty and advance sustainable operations.

4.2 Strategies in Green Marketing

Green marketing conveys corporate commitment to sustainability and leverages purchases through eco-branding and eco-labeling. Eco-branding links brand identity to sustainability, informing consumers about ethical manufacturing and resource efficiency. Eco-labels, often certified by independent bodies, signify adherence to eco-standards, aiding product differentiation and building consumer trust. Key components of green marketing include designing sustainable products using reusable materials and environmentally sound processes, setting affordable yet profitable prices to reach a broader customer base, and promoting products by focusing authentically on ecological and quality features to prevent greenwashing.

Digital marketing strategies, including social media, content marketing, and influencer collaborations, significantly enhance awareness and participation for sustainable products. Interactive digital campaigns allow consumers to engage with eco-challenges and learn about product lifecycles. Data analytics helps businesses monitor engagement and adapt to green consumer trends. By integrating eco-branding, ethical design, efficient promotion, and digital outreach, companies build trust, encourage responsible consumption, and strengthen their market competitiveness in the environmentally friendly sector.

Green Consumer Segmentation Pyramid

Green consumer segmentation pyramid categorizes consumers based on the degree of their environmental concern and environmentally sustainable purchase behavior. It assists companies to develop business plans that resonate with new attitudes that different buyers have towards environmentally friendly products. True Greens (Top Tier): Will go out of their way to be green and buy environmentally-friendly products, and promote green ideologies. Light Greens: Buy some environmental cause products at times but will prioritize price and convenience; equally as likely to buy some green products. Sprouts: They are interested on sustainability but no commitment; the choices they make are determined by the social influence and availability. Skeptical concerning green claims; have the feelings that eco-products are either very costly or ineffective. Unconcerned (Base Tier): Are least concerned with sustainability; prioritize on price and functionality of product whereas environmental impact is not of much consideration.

Green Consumer Segmentation Pyramid

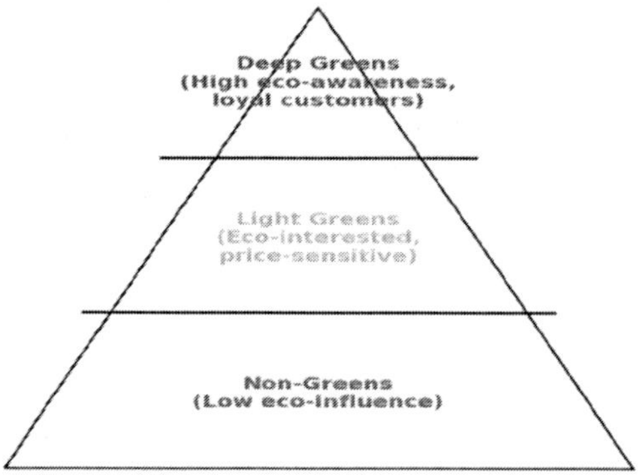

4.3 Measuring Marketing Sustainability

Effective evaluation of green marketing necessitates a methodology incorporating marketer-related and sustainability-related metrics. Customer Lifetime Value (CLV) should be adjusted to include customers' eco-friendly behaviors and commitment to sustainable brands, considering repeat purchases, advocacy, and responsiveness to sustainability initiatives. Beyond CLV, brand equity metrics are crucial, reflecting how sustainability efforts influence consumer perception, trust, and desire, thereby establishing a competitive edge. Consumer perception measures attitudes toward green products, the credibility of green claims, and overall satisfaction. Companies should also assess the environmental footprint of marketing activities by considering resource use, emissions, and waste throughout the product lifecycle and promotional processes, utilizing tools like life cycle assessment and carbon calculators. Integrating perceptual, environmental, and financial indicators provides a multidimensional view of marketing sustainability. Monitoring sustainable CLV, brand equity, consumer opinion, and environmental impact enables evidence-based decisions that support green marketing objectives, enhance stakeholder confidence, and foster responsible long-term growth.

4.4 Case Studies in Green Marketing

Green marketing campaigns offer practical insights into best practices and potential pitfalls. Leading brands like Patagonia and Tesla have successfully integrated sustainability to boost brand equity and consumer loyalty, while Unilever demonstrates the compatibility of profitable growth and sustainable marketing. Conversely, greenwashing failures, such as Volkswagen's emissions fraud and misleading claims by some fast-fashion brands, highlight the severe reputational, financial, and legal damage from unethical marketing. Effective green marketing requires structural commitment to sustainability, measurable impact, and believable communication, with authenticity building long-term brand reputation, whereas misleading claims incur significant costs. **Source**: Peattie, K., & Crane, A. (2005). "Green Marketing: Legend, Myth, Farce or Prophesy?" Qualitative Market Research, 8(4), 357–370.Critical review of green marketing strategies and their real impact.Ottman, J. A. (2011). The New Rules of Green Marketing: Strategies, Tools, and Inspiration for Sustainable Branding. Berrett-Koehler.

The Dual Approach (Finance + Marketing Integration)

5.1 Linking Sustainable Finance with Green Marketing

Organizations can integrate economic performance with environmental and social responsibility through sustainable funding and green marketing. Evaluating how sustainability marketing campaigns boost long-term profitability and brand equity addresses financial concerns. Companies that incorporate sustainability metrics into their financial models gain accountability for the financial impact of green programs, such as increased customer loyalty, improved reputation, and reduced risk from environmental compliance. Green marketing campaigns can be measured by a Return on Investment (ROI) indicator that expands traditional methods to include indirect costs, intangible direct sales, revenue, brand recognition, consumer confidence, and market distinction. Investments in eco-friendly labeling, packaging, or online campaigns promoting environmental responsibility can yield financial and social benefits, creating dual value.

5.2Corporate Strategies for Responsible Growth:

Responsible organizational growth requires embedding sustainability into corporate strategy via innovation, technology, and cross-functional alignment. Embracing a circular economy model, focused on resource efficiency and waste reduction, is essential. Models like product-as-a-service and recycling, supported by sustainable finance, enable investment in green marketing and attract ethical investors. Financial institutions increasingly favor sustainable companies, necessitating credible, quantifiable marketing strategies. Sustainable finance and green marketing highlight environmental responsibility as both an ethical imperative and a strategic investment for optimal resource use, stakeholder value, and competitive advantage, contingent on regular financial impact assessments. Technology, including AI for supply chain optimization and blockchain for transparent reporting, is a critical enabler, alongside fintech innovations like green bonds and sustainability-linked loans for improved capital allocation to impactful projects. Integrating finance and marketing through cross-functional strategies is vital for embedding sustainability. Finance can incorporate ESG indicators and assess green campaign ROI, while marketing can refine claims and boost brand value. This alignment ensures capital, product, and promotional efforts are synergistic, converting responsible actions into tangible financial and social results. Organizations can achieve strategic sustainability by adopting circular economy principles, utilizing technology, and promoting cross-organizational collaboration to mitigate risks, drive innovation, attract investment, and build customer trust for sustained, responsible growth.

Table 5: Global ESG Assets Under Management (AUM) (2020–2023)

Year	ESG AUM (USD Trillion)	Share of Total AUM (%)
2020	35.0	36%
2021	38.6	39%
2022	40.5	41%

2023	44.0	44%

Interpretation: ESG assets under management grew from USD 35 trillion in 2020 to USD 44 trillion in 2023, rising to 44% of global AUM. This expansion indicates growing institutional and retail investor alignment with responsible and sustainable financial practices.

Table 6: Consumer Willingness to Pay Premium for Sustainable Products (2020–2023)

Year	**Global Consumers Willing to Pay Extra (%)**
2020	55%
2021	60%
2022	66%
2023	71%

Interpretation:: The proportion of consumers willing to pay more for sustainable products rose from 55% in 2020 to 71% in 2023. This demonstrates increasing eco-consciousness, providing opportunities for green marketing strategies and premium sustainable product positioning.

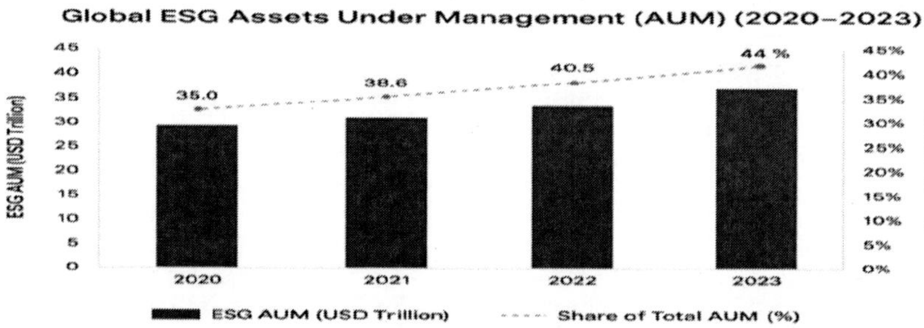

5.3 Policy and Global Perspectives: Policy frameworks and institutional structures are vital for promoting sustainability. Key actors like the UN, World Bank, and EU define global agendas and regulatory environments, exemplified by the UN's SDGs, World Bank's climate finance, and the EU Green Deal. Corporate actions are increasingly driven by sustainability regulations (e.g., ESG, carbon reporting) and voluntary disclosures (e.g., TCFD), which reduce legal risks and enhance market access. Developed economies often lead in regulatory infrastructure and green finance, while emerging markets possess significant growth potential despite resource constraints. International cooperation, tailored policy support, and capacity building are necessary to bridge these disparities and foster global sustainability.

Source: Geissdoerfer, M., Savaget, P., Bocken, N. M., &Hultink, E. J. (2017). “The Circular Economy – A New Sustainability Paradigm?” Journal of Cleaner Production, 143, 757–768.Tapscott, D., & Tapscott, A. (2016). Blockchain Revolution: How the Technology Behind Bitcoin Is Changing Money, Business, and the World. Penguin.

Future Directions

6.1 Challenges and Barrie: Companies face challenges in sustainable finance and green marketing, notably the risk of greenwashing, where overemphasis or false claims about environmental initiatives erode trust and create reputational and legal risks. Another significant hurdle is the price versus profitability dilemma. The substantial initial investment required for sustainable practices, such as alternative energy or green materials, clashes with short-term financial demands. Small and medium-sized enterprises (SMEs) are particularly affected by a lack of access to green finance and subsidies, making it difficult to justify the upfront costs of adopting sustainable business models. Consumer skepticism, fueled by greenwashing scandals, hinders responsible development by eroding trust in corporate sustainability claims. To overcome this, companies must demonstrate transparency, report quantified impact, and obtain third-party certifications to validate environmental assertions. Integrating sustainability into corporate strategy requires addressing these challenges through regulatory oversight to curb predatory practices, innovative financial instruments to ease the burden, and authentic engagement to rebuild consumer confidence. By understanding and tackling these impediments, businesses can foster greater accountability and make more credible contributions to sustainable development.

6.2 The Future of Sustainable Finance and Green Marketing: The finance and marketing sectors are being redefined by carbon-neutral markets, impact investing, and regenerative marketing, all driven by technological innovation and a global focus on climate action. Key technologies like AI, big data, and blockchain are crucial for assessing environmental impact, improving supply chains, and ensuring transparency in ESG reporting. Businesses must integrate these trends into their strategic planning, viewing sustainability as a value driver and aligning marketing with authentic environmental messaging to gain a competitive advantage and meet net-zero commitments.

6.3 Results and Discussions: This study demonstrates that sustainable finance and green marketing are mutually reinforcing drivers of responsible growth. Financial markets are increasingly integrating sustainability, with ESG investments and climate-linked instruments expanding rapidly, especially in developed economies. Green marketing success hinges on "deep green" consumer adoption, with mainstream growth dependent on transparency, affordability, and trust, underscoring the need for regulatory oversight to counter greenwashing. Businesses that synergize sustainable finance (e.g., green bonds) and marketing (e.g., eco-branding) achieve stronger consumer loyalty, better capital access, competitive advantage, and long-term resilience. While developed nations advance towards carbon-neutrality, developing countries face hurdles, though technology like AI and blockchain is enhancing transparency and trust across these domains.

6.4 Conclusion and Way Forward: The text describes a shift in organizational strategy driven by green marketing and sustainable finance, where financial decisions must align with environmental and social responsibility. Concepts like the Triple Bottom Line, ESG, and green bonds underscore sustainability as vital for long-term success. Financial leaders are tasked with directing capital to sustainable projects, while marketing leaders must build authentic narratives and prevent greenwashing. Both roles are critical for stakeholder value and achieving sustainable development goals. The paper suggests a collaborative approach involving academia (interdisciplinary research), practitioners (transparency, technology, stakeholder engagement), and policymakers (regulations, incentives) to foster regenerative, inclusive, and climate-resilient economic growth through the integration of sustainable finance and green marketing.

Source: European Commission. (2019). The European Green Deal. European Union Publications.United Nations Environment Programmed (UNEP). (2021). Finance for Nature: A Global Plan for Investments in Nature. United Nations. World Bank. (2020). Transformative Climate Finance: A New Approach for Climate Action. World Bank Publications.

References:

1. Aaker, D. A. (2020). Creating signature stories: Strategic messaging that energizes, persuades and inspires. Morgan James Publishing.

2. Bocken, N. M. P., Short, S. W., Rana, P., & Evans, S. (2014). A literature and practice review to develop sustainable business model archetypes. Journal of Cleaner Production, 65, 42–56. https://doi.org/10.1016/j.jclepro.2013.11.039
3. Carroll, A. B., & Brown, J. A. (2018). Corporate social responsibility: A review of current concepts, research, and issues. Business & Society, 57(1), 7–34. https://doi.org/10.1177/0007650318794999
4. Clark, G., Feiner, A., & Viehs, M. (2015). From the stockholder to the stakeholder: How sustainability can drive financial outperformance. Oxford University Research.
5. Elkington, J. (1997). Cannibals with forks: The triple bottom line of 21st century business. Capstone.
6. Freeman, R. E., Harrison, J. S., Wicks, A. C., Parmar, B. L., & de Colle, S. (2010). Stakeholder theory: The state of the art. Cambridge University Press.
7. Friede, G., Busch, T., & Bassen, A. (2015). ESG and financial performance: Aggregated evidence from more than 2000 empirical studies. Journal of Sustainable Finance & Investment, 5(4), 210–233. https://doi.org/10.1080/20430795.2015.1118917
8. Ginsberg, J. M., & Bloom, P. N. (2004). Choosing the right green marketing strategy. MIT Sloan Management Review, 46(1), 79–84.
9. Kotler, P., & Armstrong, G. (2021). Principles of marketing (18th ed.). Pearson.
10. Kotler, P., & Keller, K. L. (2016). Marketing management (15th ed.). Pearson.
11. Kumar, V., & Polonsky, M. J. (2017). Green marketing: A strategic approach. Business Horizons, 60(5), 659–661.
12. OECD. (2020). Green finance and investment: Sustainable infrastructure for low-carbon development in Central Asia and the Caucasus. OECD Publishing.
13. Porter, M. E., & Kramer, M. R. (2011). Creating shared value. Harvard Business Review, 89(1–2), 62–77.
14. United Nations. (2015). Transforming our world: The 2030 Agenda for Sustainable Development. United Nations.

Hybrid Entrepreneurship: Synthesize Employment and Self Employment in India

Dr. Pallavi (PhD), Associate Professor, Army Institute of Management and Technology, Greater Noida, India
Dr. Karishma Chaudhary (PhD), Academic Research Fellow Associate, University of South Africa- Florida Campus, Department of Industrial Engineering, School of Engineering, College of Science, Engineering and Technology.
Dr. Pragya Singh(PhD) , Assistant Professor, Symbiosis Centre for Management Studies, Symbiosis International University (Deemed), Noida, India

1. Introduction to Hybrid Entrepreneurship

An entrepreneurial mindset has the ability to identify opportunities, take risks, and push ideas through to reality. Entrepreneurial skills can be applied within or outside the organization, in profit or non-profit enterprises, and in business or non business activities for the purpose of bringing forward innovative thoughts. Thus, entrepreneurship is an amalgamated notion that infuses an individual to pursue opportunities in an innovative way.

Business successes can be credited to entrepreneurship. However, it may seem lucrative but an entrepreneur is exposed to financial uncertainties (Hall & Woodward, June 2010) (Iyigun & Owen, 1998). Few individuals have the ability to identify opportunities but are reluctant to switch to full-time entrepreneurship due to fear of failure and forgoing the existing income source. "Hybrid Entrepreneurship" is an entrepreneurial revolution that has been started to lower the risk of entrepreneurship entry. This revolution will continue to be powerful in the next century as the Industrial Revolution way back in the twentieth century. This concept is all about managing your venture till the time you gain experience and knowledge of any field and having full-time employment as well to sustain your living expenses.

Hybrid Entrepreneurship is the process where an individual starts his venture simultaneously with his/her wage work. Therefore, the individual can test and develop his entrepreneurial skills and learn about the venture's potential (Folta et. al., 2010).

Earlier researchers regarded Entrepreneurship as a binary choice. Either you start your own venture or settle with salary employment (Gartner, 1988). However, the introduction of hybrid entrepreneurs is in the limelight which rebuffs conventional entrepreneurial alternative concepts (Evans, 1989) as they do not have to select between salary employment and self-employment anymore (Petrova, 2012).

This strategy is good for those individuals who prefer to fulfill their employment responsibilities, and simultaneously prefer to test the waters of a new venture. This sort of approach is a great idea for those individuals who intend to reduce their burden while uncovering their untapped **competencies** (Folta et. al., 2010).

2. BACKGROUND

2.1 Evolution of Hybrid Entrepreneurship

The role and responsibilities of Entrepreneurs have been changing over time as depicted by Figure 2.

Figure 2- (Source: Author's Construction) Evolution of Entrepreneurship

In the Earliest period, the definition of entrepreneurship began when Marco Polo came to the Middle East for trade and signed an agreement with the capitalists to sell their products. During the Middle Ages, an entrepreneur was one who controlled a big production project using the resources provided by the government. In this case, the entrepreneurs were not exposed to any risks but had authority over construction and development works such as public buildings and churches. A typical entrepreneur in middle age was the priest. In the 17th century, the entrepreneurs used to sign a contract agreement with the government to provide a service or supply products that have been determined. Hence, they were liable to provide goods and services and were exposed to risks. In the 18th century, the person with capital was distinguished from the one who required capital resources. The reason for this distinction was the industrialization occurring throughout the world. In the 19th and 20th centuries, Entrepreneurs were not always associated with management. According to Merriam-Webster's online dictionary, an entrepreneur is one who organizes, manages, and assumes the risk of a business or an enterprise. The entrepreneur organizes and manages any enterprise for personal gain. The materials consumed in the business, for the use of the land, the services he employs, and the capital he requires. In the middle of the 20th Century, the function of the entrepreneurs was to recreate or revolutionize the pattern of production by introducing an invention. Innovation, the act of introducing some new ideas, was one of the most difficult tasks for the entrepreneur. In the 21st century, Entrepreneurs are known as heroes of the Free Enterprise market. Entrepreneur of the century created many products and services and is willing to face a lot of risks in the business. According to Kuratko & Hodgetts, most people say entrepreneurs are pioneers in creating new businesses. In the year 2005 Hisrich, Peter, and Shepherd regarded entrepreneurs as an organizer who controls, systematizes, purchases raw materials, arranges infrastructure, throws in their own inventiveness, and expertise, and plans and administers the venture. The future of entrepreneurship will be growth associated with upcoming technologies. Modern technologies and the internet have improved the ways of conducting business. Entrepreneurs now have the luxury of putting their business idea into action through the click of a button.

The risks involved in entrepreneurial ventures lead us to assume that it is likely that people will be deterred from engaging fully in entrepreneurial activities. Although a new Entrepreneurial revolution has been started to lower the risk of entrepreneurship entry i.e., "Hybrid Entrepreneurship". This revolution will continue to be powerful in the next century as the Industrial Revolution way back in the twentieth century. This concept is all about managing your venture till the time you gain experience and knowledge of any field and having full-time employment as well to sustain your living expenses. (Folta et. al., 2010).

2.2 Definitions and meanings of Entrepreneurship, Hybrid Entrepreneurship, and part-time entrepreneurship

Typically, individuals are either classified as entrepreneurs or non-entrepreneurs (Gartner, 1988). But with the advancement of the field, researchers were focused on an in-depth understanding of the entrepreneurial process. Researchers focused on carrying out comparative studies about entrepreneurs and non-entrepreneurs, acknowledging the differentiation and enormous variety of both groups (Bögenhold, 2018). Still, the concept and notion of Hybrid entrepreneurship groups were overlooked. The comparison between the classic notion of entrepreneurship and the modern concept of hybrid entrepreneurship is given in the table below:

Table 1: The comparison between the classic notion of entrepreneurship and the modern concept of Hybrid entrepreneurship

Entrepreneurship	**Hybrid Entrepreneurship**
Works full time as an entrepreneur	Working a full-time job while building a venture part-time
Risk-taker	Risk-averse
Legalized	Risk of being caught by employer
Work can be aligned easily	Work may not align
Invest more time to build a network	Employment contacts may be used

Source: Author's Construction

The term "Hybrid Entrepreneur" has been described in a variety of ways yet no consensus has been arrived at on the precise skills and abilities that make a person a hybrid entrepreneur. Risking and leaving a stable and secure job in order to pursue the desire of starting a new venture from the ground up may be a huge dream for some, but it is not for everyone. But hybrid entrepreneurs can reduce the risks associated with job loss while still pursuing their business (Folta et. al., 2010). This strategy entails the individual's preference to be a full-time entrepreneur in the future once the venture is profitable. Therefore, it helps to test to see if the start-up venture matches the individual's abilities, as well as learn about the venture's upside potential. This is a great approach for people who want to limit their submerged commitment while discovering their unknown abilities. (Folta et. al., 2010)

(Folta et. al., 2010) indicated that many previous researchers identified two reasons why hybrid entrepreneurship should be distinguished from entrepreneurship in general. Firstly, the hybrid strategy provides an entry point into self-employment in the future. A positive indication about potential prospects will motivate the hybrid entrepreneur to leave his wage work, whereas a negative indication will provoke the hybrid entrepreneur to abandon the quest for running a venture and continue the wage work. If no compelling indication is evident, the hybrid entrepreneur may carry on with the hybrid strategy. Secondly, researchers presented three main theoretical motives for why hybrid entrepreneurship may be methodically dissimilar from those that lead to self-employment or remain in wage-work.

Fig.1 Source: (Folta et. al., 2010) Theoretical reasons: Why hybrid entrepreneurship different from self-employment

Theoretical reason 1: A path to supplementary income is apparent that motivates an individual to start a venture along with wage work in order to earn extra money. It implies that hybrid entrepreneurs are working two jobs

Theoretical reason 2: A path to non-monetary benefits refers to those individuals taking on secondary jobs to obtain non-monetary benefits that they otherwise would not have had the opportunity to get at their ordinary wage work.

Theoretical reason 3: A path to transition is the last rationale, showing that a hybrid business strategy can provide individuals with a safe transition to self-employment. With a constant connection to paid work, hybrid entrepreneurs can manage uncertainty while experiencing what it's like to run their own businesses. With experience and information, they are adventurous in starting a business, they always have the possibility to grow or leave (Folta et. al., 2010)

Another concept that interchangeably is used in place of hybrid entrepreneurship is called part-time entrepreneurship. A part-time entrepreneur is one who works a regular job while also running his or her own business (Petrova, 2012). Part-time entrepreneurs pose the question, however, why are they so prevalent? Some other research indicates that the main motivation to be a part-time entrepreneur is not the financial capital, which craves for compensating a lower salary whereas human capital craves accumulating knowledge. (Petrova, 2012). This concept is also remarkably interesting to us as we believe that many members of our interest group can use this approach. People with this part-timer type are looking for an intellectual supplement rather than making money. Therefore, we can use them to compare with hybrid entrepreneurs. Considering the above information, there are key differences between the two. The purpose of hybrid entrepreneurship is to test your idea with as little personal risk as possible. This way, he/she can understand the possibilities of the new business idea and business as well as gain insight into what it is like to be an entrepreneur. If the business is successful, the hybrid businessman has succeeded step by step in building the business without worrying about no income, he will go to work for a salary, and during this time he has gradually worked harder on the business until he finally can quit a salaried job and become a full-time entrepreneur. Compare this strategy with the part-time entrepreneur; the difference is evident in the intentions of each individual. Part-time entrepreneurs aim to supplement their existing paid jobs with an exhilarating intellectual challenge. This means that the individual never intends to pursue a career as an entrepreneur, but rather to stick with a salaried job while being able to satisfy other interests with a side business. (Hammarström & Nylén, 2014).

3. MAIN FOCUS OF THE CHAPTER

3.1 Characteristics of Hybrid Entrepreneur

Hybrid entrepreneurs are definitely not the risk takers. But they have certain unique characteristics as follows:

According to (Folta et. al., 2010) and (Petrova, 2012) the decision of half and half passage is probably going to be related with hazard avoidance and worries about vulnerability. Individuals who consolidate a salaried occupation with business proprietorship take lower gambles than individuals who are independently employed. Since mixtures take lower gambles than full-time business visionaries, they are probably going to begin more modest, less productive organizations than their full-time partners. Moreover, People might pick a middle way to test their thoughts, find out about the enterprising system, test their capacities as business visionaries, and lessen opportunity costs from losing the pay from their ongoing work position. Half breed passage into business permits them to safeguard their assets from taking a chance with people who seem to participate in crossover business ventures to try out business thoughts and to acquire insight in business. In nations where pay rates are low, representatives are bound to take part in half breed business to expand their profit. Absence of pioneering experience: Individuals who pick crossover passage into business ventures will more often than not have high broad human resources, yet low human resources well defined for business ventures. The learning-by-doing through the decision of specific activities supplies half breeds with new data and information about business. It gives admittance to significant substantial and theoretical assets. This growing experience diminishes apparent vulnerability and improves individual and business execution. Acquired business possession experience and worked on apparent abilities in business the board during cross breed business venture expands the chances of becoming independently employed (Folta et. al., 2010)found that people with the highest switch over cost choose wage work, while those with the least choose self-employment. Only those with medium switch over costs choose hybrid entrepreneurship. Folta et al. (2010) argue that hybrid entry permits them to lower career-switching costs by remain flexible and maintaining links with the employer.

Hybrid entrepreneurship is a low-risk way to gain entrepreneurial experience and learn about business leadership. Testing a business concept in the market is a good strategy. Market feedback allows entrepreneurs to make informed decisions about choosing options, growing their business, and becoming a full-time entrepreneur.

3.2 Motives behind individuals' choice to have parallel business employment careers (Hybrid Entrepreneurship)

Entrepreneurs are creative people. The need for self-actualization, manifested in the need for achievement, forces him to create something new, new products, new ways, new sources of raw materials, new markets, and so on. Behavior is always triggered and never spontaneous. Human behavior is directed towards goals or satisfaction of needs. Whenever a person feels a need, they feel uncomfortable, and tension begins to build up in their minds. Entrepreneurs are creative people. The need for self-actualization, which manifests in the need for achievement, forces him to create something new, new products, new ways, new sources of raw materials, new markets, and so on. Hence, Entrepreneurial behavior is the result of entrepreneurial motivation to become a hybrid entrepreneur.

Several studies have been undertaken to identify factors that encourage people to start their own enterprises while working full-time employment. A survey was conducted on 262 Swedish hybrid entrepreneurs. The findings revealed that (1) The potential to work on something one is thrilled about is the most compelling reason for blending work with a side company. (2) Passion is more likely to be the driving force behind the hybrid form among people who are older when it comes to starting a business. (3) Individuals who spend additional time on the business are less likely to have enthusiasm as a driving force behind the hybrid form. (Thorgren, Nordström, & Wincent, 2014).

Another study was conducted in South Africa on a sample of 83 staff members from different industries. The results indicated that the participants are driven to hybrid entrepreneurship by both the desire to supplement salary and to derive non-monetary advantages such as passion. These two factors or motives were the most significant factors. (Dzomonda & Fatoki, 2018).

As per (Dzomonda & Fatoki, 2018) career shift strategy is not a purpose behind becoming a hybrid entrepreneur. The organizational policy was found as an impediment other than motivation by several because most policies do not support hybrid entrepreneurship. Participants were encouraged to bring their company to market to test the feasibility of their ideas while having the opportunity to learn about the dynamics of the industry. (Dzomonda & Fatoki, 2018)

Another study indicated that some individuals opt for hybrid entrepreneurs along with their full-time employment as they have enough free time to do business along with their salary employment (Solesvik, March 2017). Another study indicated that hybrid entrepreneurs open up a side business to focus on their interests or build their interests (Renna, 2006). Another study in Indonesia indicated that the motive to become a hybrid entrepreneur are internal and external factors that enable someone to have a wage job while working on their own business, and why they stay in this role. (Indudewi, 2015). Another research also found that individuals may choose to remain in the hybrid model if the entrepreneurship/employment combination offers similar or better opportunities for self-fulfilment. Therefore, based on literature motivations that might explain a person's entry into hybrid entrepreneurship are:

Monetary benefits: According to the study by Folta et al. (2010), one of the primary motivations for individuals to engage in parallel business employment careers is monetary benefits. By having additional income streams, individuals can increase their overall earning potential, reduce financial dependence on a single job or employer, and improve their financial security and stability.

Psychological benefits: Parallel business employment careers can also provide psychological benefits to individuals. Pursuing different careers can provide a sense of accomplishment, personal growth, and fulfillment that may not be possible in a single career. It can also provide a sense of autonomy and control over one's career and professional development.

Learning about the potential venture: Engaging in parallel business employment careers can also provide individuals with the opportunity to learn about potential ventures or industries they may be interested in pursuing in the future. This can help individuals gain valuable knowledge, skills, and experience that can be applied to future entrepreneurial endeavors.

Work schedule flexibility: Parallel business employment careers can also offer individuals greater work schedule flexibility, allowing them to balance their personal and professional commitments more effectively. This can be particularly beneficial for individuals with caregiving responsibilities or those who wish to pursue other interests outside of work.

Perceived environmental uncertainty: Lastly, perceived environmental uncertainty is another motivation for individuals to engage in parallel business employment careers. By having multiple income streams and diverse skills, individuals can better navigate uncertain economic conditions or changes in their primary industry or job market.

Non-monetary benefits such as the pursuit of passion or hobby: According to a study by Folta et al. (2010), individuals may choose to have parallel business employment careers not solely for financial reasons but also for the non-monetary benefits. This can include the opportunity to pursue their passion or engage in a hobby that they are passionate about. By having parallel careers, individuals can allocate time and resources towards activities that bring them joy and fulfillment outside of their primary employment.

Economic hardship: Economic hardship is a common motivation for individuals to engage in parallel business employment careers. During times of economic instability or recession, individuals may face difficulties in finding stable employment or maintaining a steady income. Having parallel careers can help mitigate the impact of economic hardship by diversifying income sources and providing a safety net during challenging times.

Negative income shocks: Negative income shocks refer to unexpected events or circumstances that result in a significant decrease in income. This could include job loss, reduction in work hours, or a decline in business revenue. By having parallel business employment careers, individuals can better cope with negative income shocks as they have alternative income streams to rely on, reducing the financial impact of such shocks.

Supplementary income: Supplementary income refers to additional income earned through parallel business employment careers alongside a primary job or source of income. This additional income can provide individuals with financial security, allowing them to meet their needs, save for the future, or pursue other financial goals. Supplementary income can also provide individuals with more financial freedom and flexibility, allowing them to afford certain luxuries or investments that may not be possible with a single income source.

To test entrepreneurial waters: Possibility to become self-employed to learn more about the potential of a company and the endurance level of an individual as an entrepreneur (Folta et. Al., 2010). Figure 3 summarizes the motives to be a hybrid entrepreneur.

In summary, individuals may choose to have parallel business employment careers for various reasons, including monetary benefits, psychological benefits, learning opportunities, work schedule flexibility, and perceived environmental uncertainty. As well as non-monetary benefits like pursuing passions or hobbies, coping with economic hardship and negative income shocks, as well as earning supplementary income to enhance financial stability and flexibility.

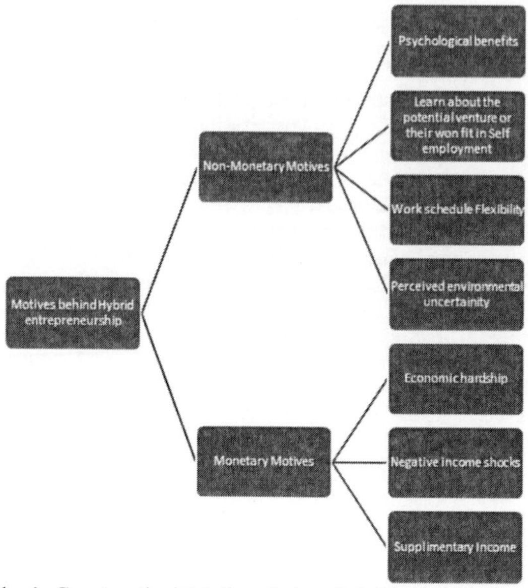

Figure 4: Source (Author's Construction) Motives to be a hybrid entrepreneur

3.3 Challenges faced by Hybrid Entrepreneurs

There are many challenges faced by hybrid entrepreneurs. Hybrid entrepreneurs have to multitask, wear multiple hats and definitely explore the unknowns. Eventually, they come across various challenges.

- **Less time for their venture:** By definition, hybrids have salaried jobs. Having a job means that they have less time at their disposal for their businesses. The job is likely to provide them with a fixed monthly salary. If conditions and circumstances wear them down, their enthusiasm for hybrid entrepreneurship is likely to wane. Hybrid entrepreneurs that devote a significant amount of time to their firm may find it difficult to maintain their enthusiasm due to issues with role conflicts, stress management, and achieving a work-life balance. (Hammarström & Nylén, 2014)
- **Longer Gestation period**: As per the research conducted previously infer that, hybrids do not place an emphasis on progress in the company gestation phase. As a result, we anticipate them to be less likely to attain vital company milestones like first sales, first transaction, first profit, and, most importantly, first employment. As a result, hybrids are less likely than full-time entrepreneurs to accomplish key stages in the company development process, take less risk, and launch smaller enterprises. Hybrids are not financially dependent on their enterprises. They can afford to keep marginally profitable small firms alive. As a result, we expect hybrid enterprises to last longer than businesses launched by full-time entrepreneurs. (Kritskaya et.al., 2017)
- **Start small ventures:** Hybrids have limited time at their disposal, and therefore start smaller ventures, less likely to be corporations and businesses with partners. Hybrids are more likely to start businesses from scratch rather than acquire businesses. Businesses

started by hybrids are small, and have lower sales, labor costs and earnings than businesses started by full-time entrepreneurs. (Kritskaya et.al., 2017)

- Hybrid entrepreneurs report significant lower accumulated sales, accumulated labor costs and accumulated earnings than full-time entrepreneurs. (Kritskaya et.al., 2017)

3.4 Mode of Entry into Hybrid Entrepreneurship

In this section, we will explore the hybrid entrepreneurship entry modes. Entrepreneurship entrance modes include founding a new enterprise (new venture start-up) or taking over an existing firm. (Cooper & Dunkelberg, 1986). Another study on entry mode into hybrid Entrepreneurship was conducted, it claimed that hybrid entrepreneurs choose either new venture start-up or Business takeover. These modes of entering hybrid entrepreneurship and their characteristics are shown in Table 1 Type of entry into Hybrid entrepreneurship" Each approach of market entry has advantages and disadvantages. Entrepreneurs need to evaluate their options to choose the entry mode that best suits their strategy and goals.

Table No.2: Mode of Entry into Hybrid Entrepreneurship.

Type of entry	Advantages	Disadvantages
New Enterprise Start-up	• Allow more flexibility • Independence • Personal fulfilment • Agility	• Financial risk • Time commitment • More Responsibility • Instability • Risk of failure • Sometimes it takes longer time to access the market
Existing Business Takeover	• Reduced entry barriers • Customer prior knowledge of the venture start-ups • Present access to logistics, • Existing access to employees • Existing access to distribution channels • Less risky and uncertain • Avoid the considerable costs of setting up its own operations	• High cost involved • Existing employee morale may decrease

Source: Author's construction

New Enterprise Start-up: New enterprise start-up is typically the most used mode to enter the league of entrepreneurs, and therefore they begin their journey using this model of entry. A start-up (or start-up) is a business that is still in its early phases of growth. The advantage of this mode of entry is that enterprises enjoy flexibility to establish their venture their way. An entrepreneur enjoys independence to set up a mission and vision in the sense that this is what the venture will become in the future: into what it will grow. Another advantage of starting a new venture for the hybrid entrepreneur is to achieve personal fulfilment in terms of profit, satisfaction, autonomy to plan everything from scratch and sales as well. In terms of agility, new ventures are more agile in comparison to business takeover. In a new venture purpose is defined through thoughtful consideration of how you decide to spend time and creative supply of your solutions.

Among the disadvantages of establishing a new enterprise with full time employment is the financial risk. The risk of losing money on the investment or business endeavour is known as financial risk. Credit risk, operational risk, and liquidity risk are some of the most prevalent and different financial threats. Financial risk is a hazard that might cause interested parties to lose money. Most instances where a small firm receives start-up funding through a loan, the entrepreneur need to obtain the loan by guaranteeing the private property, such as a home. Endangering equity in one's personal assets is a financial obligation not all entrepreneurs are willing to make. Time commitment is another alarming issue as hybrid entrepreneurs spend long hours a week on another job. When an individual begins any venture, it is likely, at least in the starting, that they will have little employees. This leaves all the duties and tasks to the entrepreneur. Hybrid entrepreneurs report working more than eighty hours a week handling the whole lot of tasks from procuring to marketing themselves. This time commitment can place a pressure and burden on self and family and leads to the stress of starting a new business venture. While the business may be profitable at the start, peripheral factors such as recessions in the economy, new contenders that enter the marketplace, or fluctuations in consumer demand may halt the enterprise growth. Even entrepreneurs who undergo exhaustive planning procedures can never predict all the possible changes in the business environment.

Business Takeover: Market entry can be a costly option due to huge costs. An alternative way for hybrid entrepreneurs to enter new markets is through a business takeover. A business takeover involves **not to start a fresh start-up, but to buy and develop current businesses**. A well-established business often has brand loyalty with customers and is well-known in the market. As a new entrepreneur, you may have ideas about modifying the existing brand, but you do not need to make a big investment to build up something entirely new. By adopting this entry mode, hybrid entrepreneurs can enjoy less entry barriers. Altering a brand when you already have a loyal customer base is much easier than building a market existence from scratch.

Business takeovers are also advantageous for hybrid entrepreneurial firms that may be too small to make the needed investments to enter the new market themselves. In addition, they need not spend time to get the information about the access to logistics, employees, distribution channel etc. Even one cannot deny the fact that hybrid entrepreneurs can evade the substantial costs of setting up their own operations. Overall, business takeovers are less risky and uncertain.

The disadvantages of this entry mode, on the other hand, are the high cost involved in taking over an established business and the likelihood that existing employees' goals vary from the entrepreneur's goals.

Which entry mode a firm prefers also varies on several factors viz., the firm's size, financial strength, and the financial conditions, age of the entrepreneur, educational qualification, family size, type of position he holds in his current employment etc.

3.5 SWOT analysis to identify strengths, weaknesses, threats, and opportunities for the hybrid entrepreneurship

A SWOT analysis is used to evaluate the potential opportunities and limitations for hybrid entrepreneurship. The key difficulties (weaknesses) and benefits (strengths) for hybrid entrepreneurship were identified based on a review of scholarly literature. It resulted in proposals (possibilities) for growing hybrid entrepreneurship.

Figure 4: Source (Author's Construction) SWOT analysis of Hybrid Entrepreneurship

Hybrid entrepreneurship is especially important for young people. A recent trend has also witnessed that the number of hybrid entrepreneurs are in rise, indicating a good trend in India. It suggests that people's entrepreneurial abilities were largely utilized in hybrid entrepreneurship. The reasons are that young people are more enthusiastic and are often willing to work for extended hours to achieve entrepreneurial goals. Moreover, there are many educated people who may also help to grow more hybrid entrepreneurs. As far as the weaknesses are concerned the concept of hybrid entrepreneurship does not list in legal acts on business. However, individuals have no privileges defined for the hybrid enterprises. Whereas this field has many opportunities as the government of India provides support for developing and entrepreneurship education at all levels, there are specific programmes and grants available to help entrepreneurship to flourish further.

Further, the threats include that there is no explicit provision in Indian employment law that addresses the legality of dual work in India. In India, the punishment for multiple work is not clearly defined in the dual employment statute. It may be established from several judicial rulings that the implications of dual employment in India include the termination of the employee who has multiple occupations. Furthermore, hybrid entrepreneurs understand that their competitors are not only other small companies. There are major brands in every nook and corner across the country, which means they must contend with other local companies as well as companies with large marketing expenditures and even greater brand awareness. Larger corporations can easily overshadow hybrid entrepreneurs.

4. Conclusion Many elements influence the establishment of a hybrid entrepreneurship (individual objectives, passion, age, family size, nature of full-time work, an individual's economic situation, participation). And India has a strong potential for hybrid entrepreneurship, which is defined by the proportion of educated individuals and the potential of the youthful population. But various limiting factors like excessive time consumption when working full-time in employment and operating their own enterprise, no legislative framework to govern hybrid entrepreneurship and no support instrument to promote hybrid entrepreneurship does not drive many individuals to venture into entrepreneurship. It implies that special support instruments are required for the development of hybrid firms.

5. Key recommendations for the policy makers and educationalists

Our chapter also has significant policy implications. Policymakers who design tools to promote entrepreneurship can use our study to design their programs towards hybrid entrepreneurs. Till date, prevailing policy initiatives have ignored hybrid entrepreneurship – an important oversight, in spite of the strong increase in hybrid entrepreneurship in recent years. Apart from revising existing policy instruments, policymakers could also design programs that specifically target hybrid entrepreneurship. The government should also consider training programs that specifically target the information needs of hybrid entrepreneurs. But the training programs should be in a flexible manner as hybrid entrepreneurs get less time and flexibility in comparison to pure entrepreneurs. We anticipate that our chapter urges policymakers to better address the case of hybrid entrepreneurship and to adjust policy procedures, accordingly.

6. Key Terms and Definitions

- **Entrepreneurship:** Entrepreneurship is the process of identifying, creating, and pursuing opportunities to develop innovative ideas, products, services, or businesses. It involves the willingness to take calculated risks, the ability to think creatively, and the drive to bring ideas to fruition. Entrepreneurship encompasses a range of activities, including identifying market gaps, developing business plans, securing funding, managing resources, and navigating the complexities of starting and running a business.
- **Self-Employment:** Self-employment refers to a work arrangement in which an individual operates their own business, provides services as an independent contractor, or engages in freelance work, rather than being employed by an external organization.
- **Part time Entrepreneurship:** Part-time entrepreneurship refers to the pursuit of entrepreneurial activities while simultaneously maintaining part-time or full-time employment in another capacity.
- **Hybrid Entrepreneurship:** Hybrid Entrepreneurship refers to individuals who engage in entrepreneurial activities while also maintaining other employment or commitments. It allows individuals to pursue their entrepreneurial aspirations while mitigating some of the risks associated with full-time entrepreneurship.
- **Business Takeover:** A business takeover refers to the acquisition of a company by another entity, resulting in the transfer of control and ownership from the original owners to the acquiring party. This can involve the purchase of a majority stake or all assets of the target company, often leading to significant changes in management, operations, and strategic direction.
- **New enterprise Start-up:** A new enterprise startup refers to the process of establishing and launching a new business venture or company. This typically involves developing a business concept, securing resources, such as funding and personnel, and initiating operations with the goal of creating a sustainable and profitable business entity.

13. Keywords

Hybrid entrepreneurship, Part-time entrepreneurship, Entrepreneurs, New Enterprise Start-up, Existing Business Takeover

References

Bögenhold, D. (2018). From Hybrid Entrepreneurs to Entrepreneurial Billionaires: Observations on the Socioeconomic Heterogeneity of Self-employment. American Behavioral Scientist.

Cooper, A. C., & Dunkelberg, W. C. (1986). Entrepreneurship and paths to business ownership. Strategic Management Journal, 7, 53–68.

Dzomonda, O., & Fatoki, O. (2018). DEMYSTIFYING THE MOTIVATIONS TOWARDS . Academy of Entrepreneurship Journal, Volume 24, Issue 4, 1-9.

Evans, D. S. (1989). An estimated model of entrepreneurial choice under liquidity constraints. Journal of Political Economy, 97(4), 808–827.

Folta et. al. (2010). Hybrid Entrepreneurship. Management Science, 56(2),, p. 253-269.

Gartner, W. B. (1988). "Who is an entrepreneur?" is the wrong question. American Journal of Small Business, 12(4), 11–32.

Hall, R. E., & Woodward, S. E. (June 2010). The Burden of the Nondiversifiable Risk of Entrepreneurship. American Economic Review, VOL. 100, NO. 3,, pp. 1163-94.

Hammarström, N., & Nylén, V. (2014). A study about identifying influencing factors correlated to academic entrepreneurship. . Umeå School of Business and Economics .

Indudewi, F. Y. (2015). Success Factors of Hybrid Entrepreneurs: . Mediterranean Journal of Social Sciences , 84-90.

Iyigun, M., & Owen, A. (1998). Risk, entrepreneurship, and human-capital. American Economic Review, 88(2), p. 454-457.

Kritskaya et.al. (2017). Hybrid Entrepreneurs: Characteristics and Achievements. Entreprendre & Innover, 7-19.

Petrova, K. (2012). Part-time entrepreneurship and 俫nancial constraints: Evidence from the panel study of entrepreneurial dynamics. . Small Business Economics, 39(2), 473–493.

Renna, F. (2006). Moonlighting and Overtime: A Cross-Country Analysis. Journal of Labor,Vol. 27 No. 4, pp. 575-591.

Solesvik, M. Z. (March 2017). Hybrid Entrepreneurship:. Technology Innovation Management Review, (Volume 7, Issue 3), 34-41.

Thorgren, S., Nordström, C., & Wincent, J. (2014). Hybrid entrepreneurship: the importance of passion. Baltic Journal of Management, Vol. 9 No. 3, 314-329.